Best Easy Day Hikes
Springfield, Illinois

Help Us Keep This Guide Up to Date

Every effort has been made by the author and editors to make this guide as accurate and useful as possible. However, many things can change after a guide is published—trails are rerouted, regulations change, facilities come under new management, etc.

We would appreciate hearing from you concerning your experiences with this guide and how you feel it could be improved and kept up to date. While we may not be able to respond to all comments and suggestions, we'll take them to heart and we'll also make certain to share them with the author. Please send your comments and suggestions to the following address:

GPP
Reader Response/Editorial Department
P.O. Box 480
Guilford, CT 06437

Or you may e-mail us at:

editorial@GlobePequot.com

Thanks for your input, and happy trails!

Best Easy Day Hikes
Springfield, Illinois

Johnny Molloy

FALCONGUIDES

GUILFORD, CONNECTICUT
HELENA, MONTANA
AN IMPRINT OF THE GLOBE PEQUOT PRESS

To buy books in quantity for corporate use
or incentives, call **(800) 962-0973**
or e-mail **premiums@GlobePequot.com**.

FALCONGUIDES®

FalconGuides is an imprint of Globe Pequot Press.
Falcon, FalconGuides, and Outfit Your Mind are registered trademarks of Morris Book Publishing, LLC.

Text design: Sheryl P. Kober
Project editor: Julie Marsh
Layout: Joanna Beyer

Maps by Design Maps Inc.
TOPO! Explorer software and SuperQuad source maps courtesy of National Geographic Maps. For information about TOPO! Explorer, TOPO!, and Nat Geo Maps products, go to www.topo.com or www.natgeomaps.com.

Library of Congress Cataloging-in-Publication Data is available on file.

ISBN 978-0-7627-7173-8

Printed in the United States of America

10 9 8 7 6 5 4 3 2 1

Contents

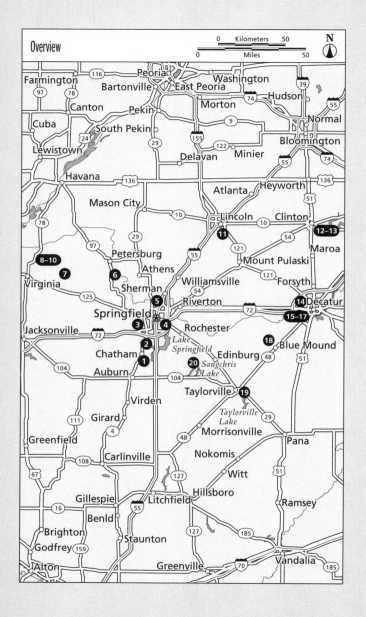

Acknowledgments

Thanks to all the people who helped me with this book, primarily the people at Falcon, including Jess Haberman and Julie Marsh. Thanks to Lafuma for their warm sleeping bags and good-fitting packs, to Delorme for their accurate Global Positioning Systems, and to Merrell for quality hiking shoes and boots. Also, thanks to all the park personnel who answered my tireless questions while trying to manage these jewels of greater Springfield. The biggest thanks go to the trail builders and hikers of the area, for without you all there wouldn't be trails in the first place.

Introduction

The astonishing view stretched to the horizon. I stood on the observation deck, where fields, farms, forests, and towns stretched to the horizon. Griswold Conservation Area, near Blue Mound, was but one of many scenic and rewarding destinations in this book. I mentally reflected on other destinations, recounting all the worthwhile hikes of greater Springfield. In town, several converted railroad grades had been turned into trails. One offered a pure urban hike used regularly by exercisers. Another presented lake views along the way. Another traveled by both lake and streamside scenery in rich woods. Two other Springfield trails explored deep woods on slender footpaths. To the west, four hikes visited a large state wildlife preserve, where alluring lakes made for wildlife-rich hike settings, as well as high hills that opened surprising vistas. New Salem had a hike into human and natural history. Other state parks held still more destinations, like the Lakeside Nature Trail and the Schoolhouse Trail, both at Weldon Springs State Park. The Hickory Lane Trail was a wooded escape at Sangchris Lake State Park. The nearby city of Decatur had a hike at historic Fairview Park within its bounds. Rock Creek Conservation Area was a gem. The Lookout Trail explored an historic homestead, along with genuine Illinois prairie. The River Trail was a personal favorite. It roamed prairies, passed by huge old growth trees, and then traveled along dark and mysterious bottoms along the Sangamon River. It even had some history too, passing an old spring bottling plant and mill site. Down south, the Lincoln Prairie Trail was a shining example of a rail trail that made the most of its setting.

With this book in hand and willing feet you can explore the greater Springfield region. No matter where you go, the trails in this book will enhance your outdoor experience and leave you appreciating the natural splendors of Central Illinois. Enjoy.

The Nature of Greater Springfield

Springfield's hiking grounds range from singletrack wooded trails along rivers to grassy prairie hikes, lakeside treks, and strolls on asphalt greenways. Hikes in this guide cover the gamut. While by definition a best easy day hike is not strenuous and generally poses little danger to the traveler, knowing a few details about the nature of greater Springfield will enhance your explorations.

Weather

Springfield certainly experiences all four seasons. Summer can be warm, with sporadic downright hot spells. Morning hikers can avoid heat and the common afternoon thunderstorms. Hiking increases when the first northerly fronts of fall sweep cool, clear air across the Land of Lincoln. Crisp mornings give way to warm afternoons. Fall is drier than summer. Winter will bring frigid, subfreezing days, chilling rains, and significant snow. However, a brisk hiking pace will keep you warm. Each cold month has a few days of mild weather. Make the most of them. Spring will be more variable. A warm day can be followed by a cold, snowy one. Extensive spring rains bring regrowth, but also keep hikers indoors and flood streams and rivers. But any avid hiker will find more good hiking days than they will have time to hike in spring and every other season.

Critters

Springfield trail treaders will encounter mostly benign creatures on these trails, such as deer, squirrels, wild turkeys, a variety of songbirds, and rabbits galore. More rarely seen (during the daylight hours especially) are coyotes, raccoons, and opossums. Deer in some of the parks are remarkably tame and may linger on or close to the trail as you approach. If you feel uncomfortable when encountering any critter, keep your distance and they will generally keep theirs.

Be Prepared

Hiking in greater Springfield is generally safe. Still, hikers should be prepared, whether they are out for a short stroll at Fairview Park or venturing into secluded sections of the Jim Edgar Panther Creek State Fish and Wildlife Area. Some specific advice:

- Bug repellent.
- Know the basics of first aid, including how to treat bleeding, bites and stings, and fractures, strains, or sprains. Pack a first-aid kit on each excursion.
- Familiarize yourself with the symptoms of heat exhaustion and heat stroke. Heat exhaustion symptoms include heavy sweating, muscle cramps, headache, dizziness, and fainting. Should you or any of your hiking party exhibit any of these symptoms, cool the victim down immediately by rehydrating and getting him or her to an air-conditioned location. Cold showers also help reduce body temperature. Heat stroke is much more serious: The victim may lose consciousness and the skin is hot and dry to the touch. In this event, call 911 immediately.

- Regardless of the weather, your body needs a lot of water while hiking. A full 32-ounce bottle is the minimum for these short hikes, but more is always better. Bring a full water bottle, whether water is available along the trail or not.

- Don't drink from streams, rivers, creeks, or lakes without treating or filtering the water first. Waterways and water bodies may host a variety of contaminants, including giardia, which can cause serious intestinal unrest.

- Prepare for extremes of both heat and cold by dressing in layers.

- Carry a backpack in which you can store extra clothing, ample drinking water and food, and whatever goodies like guidebooks, cameras, and binoculars, you might want. Consider bringing a GPS with tracking capabilities.

- Most Springfield trails have cell phone coverage, but you can never be absolutely sure until you are on location. Bring your device, but make sure you've turned it off or got it on the vibrate setting while hiking. Nothing like a "wake the dead"-loud ring to startle every creature, including fellow hikers.

- Keep children under careful watch. Trails travel along many rivers, streams, ponds, and lakes, most of which are not recommended for swimming. Hazards along some of the trails include poison ivy, uneven footing, and steep drop-offs; make sure children don't stray from the designated route. Children should carry a plastic whistle; if they become lost, they should stay in one place and blow the whistle to summon help.

Leave No Trace

Trails in Springfield and neighboring communities are well used year-round. We, as trail users, must be especially vigilant to make sure our passage leaves no lasting mark. Here are some basic guidelines for preserving trails in the region:

- Pack out all your own trash, including biodegradable items like orange peels. You might also pack out garbage left by less considerate hikers.

- Don't approach or feed any wild creatures—the ground squirrel eyeing your snack food is best able to survive if it remains self-reliant.

- Don't pick prairie wildflowers or gather rocks, antlers, feathers, and other treasures along the trail. Removing these items will only take away from the next hiker's experience.

- Avoid damaging trailside soils and plants by remaining on the established route. This is also a good rule of thumb for avoiding poison ivy and other common regional trailside irritants.

- Be courteous by not making loud noises while hiking.

- Many of these trails are multiuse, which means you'll share them with other hikers, trail runners, mountain bikers, and equestrians. Familiarize yourself with the proper trail etiquette, yielding the trail when appropriate.

- Use outhouses at trailheads or along the trail.

Springfield Area Boundaries and Corridors

For the purposes of this guide, best easy day hikes are confined to a one-hour drive from downtown Springfield and are primarily in Sangamon and Macon County, with others in Cass, Menard, Christian, and Logan counties.

Two major interstates converge in Springfield. Directions to trailheads are given from these interstates and other arteries. They include I-55, I-72, and IL 4—Veterans Parkway—which together form a loop around Springfield.

Land Management

The following government organizations manage most of the public lands described in this guide, and can provide further information on these hikes and other trails in their service areas.

- Springfield Park District, 2500 South Eleventh Street, Springfield, IL 62703; (217) 544-1751; www.spring fieldparks.org

- Macon County Conservation District, 3939 Nearing Lane, Decatur, IL 62521; (217) 423-7708; www.macon countyconservation.org

- Illinois State Parks, One Natural Resources Way, Springfield, IL 62702-1271; (217) 782-6302; www.dnr .illinois.gov/

How to Use This Guide

This guide is designed to be simple and easy to use. Each hike is described with a map and summary information that delivers the trail's vital statistics, including length, difficulty, fees and permits, park hours, canine compatibility, and trail contacts. Directions to the trailhead are also provided, along with a general description of what you'll see along the way. A detailed route finder (Miles and Directions) sets forth mileages between significant landmarks along the trail.

Hike Selection

This guide describes trails that are accessible to every hiker, whether visiting from out of town or someone lucky enough to live in greater Springfield. The hikes are no longer than 5 miles round-trip, and most are considerably shorter. They range in difficulty from flat excursions perfect for a family outing to more challenging hilly treks. While these trails are among the best, keep in mind that nearby trails, often in the same park or preserve, may offer options better suited to your needs. I've sought to space hikes throughout the greater Springfield region, so wherever your starting point, you'll find a great easy day hike nearby.

Difficulty Ratings

These are all easy hikes, but easy is a relative term. To aid in the selection of a hike that suits particular needs and abilities, each is rated easy, moderate, or more challenging. Bear in mind that even most challenging routes can be made easy by hiking within your limits and taking rests when you need them.

- **Easy** hikes are generally short and flat, taking no longer than an hour to complete.

- **Moderate** hikes involve increased distance and relatively mild changes in elevation and will take one to two hours to complete.

- **More challenging** hikes feature some steep stretches, greater distances, and generally take longer than two hours to complete.

These are completely subjective ratings—consider that what you think is easy is entirely dependent on your level of fitness and the adequacy of your gear (primarily shoes). If you are hiking with a group, you should select a hike with a rating that's appropriate for the least fit and prepared in your party.

Approximate hiking times are based on the assumption that on flat ground, most walkers average 2 miles per hour. Adjust that rate by the steepness of the terrain and your level of fitness (subtract time if you're an aerobic animal and add time if you're hiking with kids), and you have a ballpark hiking duration. Be sure to add more time if you plan to picnic or take part in other activities like bird-watching or photography.

Trail Finder

Best Hikes for Lake Lovers

1	Interurban Trail
7	Gridley Lake Loop
8	Prairie Lake Hike
12	Lakeside Nature Trail

Best Hikes for Children

4	Lost Bridge Trail
14	Fairview Park Hike
16	Lookout Trail
18	Griswold Conservation Area Vista

Best Hikes for Dogs

3	Wabash Trail
10	Governors Trail
13	Schoolhouse Trail
20	Hickory Lane Trail

Best Hikes for Great Views

1	Interurban Trail
4	Lost Bridge Trail
10	Governors Trail
18	Griswold Conservation Area Vista

Best Hikes for Solitude

2	Lick Creek Preserve Hike
6	New Salem Loop
11	Salt Creek Trail
20	Hickory Lane Trail

Best Hikes for River and Stream Lovers

Best Hikes for Nature Lovers

Map Legend

═══〈55〉═══	Interstate Highway
───〈51〉───	U.S. Highway
───〈29〉───	State Highway
───〈11〉───	County/Local Road
= = = = = =	Unpaved Road
▬▬▬▬▬▬	Featured Trail
- - - - - -	Trail
──────	Paved Trail
┼─┼─┼─┼	Railroad
～～～	River/Creek
⋯⋯	Swamp/Marsh
⬭	Body of Water
┄┄┄	State/County/Preserve
┄┄┄	National Forest/National Park
🛶	Boat Ramp
‿	Bridge
⛺	Camping
•─•	Gate
🅿	Parking
🛆	Picnic Area
■	Point of Interest/Structure
▲	Primitive Campsite
○	Town
⓫	Trailhead
⊢───⊣	Tunnel
◧	Viewpoint/Overlook
❓	Visitor/Information Center

1 Interurban Trail

The Interurban Trail is part of the growing network of interconnected paths in Springfield. This section starts in Chatham, just south of Springfield, and travels a mostly wooded corridor to meet Lake Springfield, where you can enjoy a wonderful watery view from a bridge spanning the impoundment.

Distance: 4.6-mile out-and-back
Approximate hiking time: 2.0 to 2.5 hours
Difficulty: Moderate, due to distance only
Trail surface: Asphalt
Best season: Year-round
Other trail users: Joggers, bicyclists
Canine compatibility: Leashed dogs permitted

Fees and permits: No fees or permits required
Schedule: Sunrise to sunset
Maps: Interurban Trail; USGS Chatham
Trail contacts: Springfield Park District, 2500 South Eleventh Street, Springfield, IL 62703; (217) 544-1751; www.spring fieldparks.org

Finding the trailhead: From exit 93 on I-72 southwest of downtown, take Veterans Parkway, IL 4, south for 4.5 miles to Walnut Street in Chatham. Turn left on Walnut Street and follow it a short distance to the intersection with State Street, across the street from the post office. There is public trail parking on the south side of Walnut Street. The Interurban Trail starts on the north side of Walnut. GPS Trailhead Coordinates: N39° 40.577' / W89° 42.165'

The Hike

Interestingly, this part of the Interurban Trail follows an old electric trolley car line that once connected the communities of Chatham and Springfield. A modern railroad, Union Pacific, utilized by Amtrak, runs parallel to the Interurban Trail. However, they are most often separated by a wooded corridor, and the infrequent trains don't seem to bother trail users. By the way, the Interurban Trail is used by commuters bicycling to work into the government hub that is downtown Springfield. In addition to commuters, you will see bicyclers, joggers, retirees, and mothers with strollers.

The 8-foot-wide asphalt path has virtually no elevation change, making it an easy walk. The trail stretches almost 8 miles end to end. Future plans call for the trail being extended south to Auburn. Trail difficulty is determined solely by distance. Deep, shady woods border the trail as it passes by houses in Chatham, creating a green tunnel of walnut, cherry, and other species. Newer houses and younger trees and brush characterize the trailside terrain once you leave Chatham. Redwing blackbirds will be singing in these open areas.

You are traveling down the valley of Polecat Creek, flowing toward Lake Springfield to your west. But the creek isn't visible from the trail at this point. Ahead, you will come alongside a golf course. Watch out for errant golf balls! Seriously, you will be able to observe golfers at their game.

Honeysuckle sweetens the air during the summer season, while sumac offers brilliant red in fall. The woods thicken as you come near Lake Springfield and alongside Lick Creek Preserve, a small wildland that encompasses part of the shoreline around the lake. The Polecat Creek Trail makes a half-mile loop and returns to the Interurban Trail. The singletrack natural surface path can add a half mile to your hike.

The Interurban Trail soon comes alongside Lake Springfield. Aquatic views open of the upper Lick Creek embayment. You will reach the restored rail bridge that spans Lake

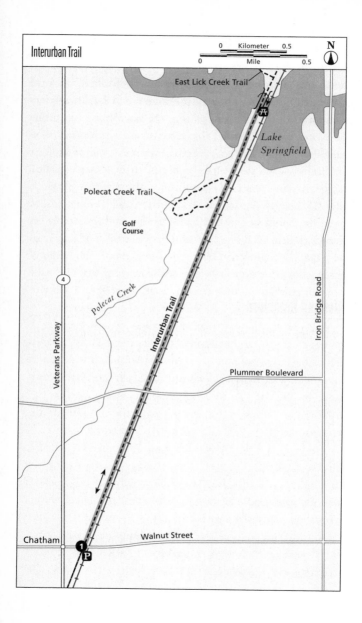

Interurban Trail

0   Kilometer   0.5
0   Mile   0.5

N

East Lick Creek Trail

Lake
Springfield

Polecat Creek Trail

Golf
Course

Polecat Creek

Interurban Trail

Plummer Boulevard

Veterans Parkway

4

Iron Bridge Road

Chatham   Walnut Street

1
P

Springfield. This bridge offers deep views into the impoundment, and is a good place to turn around. Since the impoundment extends east–west here, the bridge offers sunrise and sunset vistas. Note that a small picnic area is located just south of the bridge. If you wish to continue beyond Lake Springfield, the Interurban Trail continues following the old trolley line, and then traces the Macarthur Boulevard extension to meet the Wabash Trail, near Wabash Avenue. Bicyclists often combine the two paths together to make for a longer ride.

The Interurban Trail opened in 2004, but when Macarthur Boulevard was extended south to the interstate, the Interurban Trail was threatened. The Illinois Department of Transportation (IDOT) saw an opportunity and integrated the path into the master plan for the interstate interchange, making the connection with the Wabash Trail viable.

Miles and Directions

0.0 Pick up the Interurban Trail as it travels north, leaving Walnut Street in Chatham. Picnic tables and bike racks are situated at the trailhead.

0.7 A sidewalk leaves left and connects to a subdivision.

0.8 Plummer Boulevard dips under the path.

1.0 Come alongside a golf course to the west of the trail.

1.7 Look for a mounted tornado siren to the left of the trail.

1.9 Reach the trail kiosk and entrance to the Polecat Creek Trail. This path makes a half mile loop into the Lick Creek Preserve. The Interurban Trail stretches north on elevated fill, while wetlands drop off below.

2.2 Pass a picnic area astride the path.

2.3 Reach the railroad bridge crossing Lake Springfield. Enjoy the views of the water. Backtrack.

4.6 Return to the trailhead.

2 Lick Creek Preserve Hike

This hike encompasses two trails emanating from one trail-head. First, the West Lick Creek Trail takes you across Lick Creek through bottomlands and hills past big trees. After returning to the trailhead, you will trek the East Lick Creek Trail beneath rich forest along the shore of Lake Springfield to meet the Interurban Trail. The whole area is under the protected umbrella of the Lick Creek Preserve.

Distance: 3.8-mile double out-and-back

Approximate hiking time: 2.0 to 2.5 hours

Difficulty: Moderate, has a few hills

Trail surface: Natural surfaces

Best season: Year-round

Other trail users: Mountain bikers

Canine compatibility: Leashed dogs permitted

Fees and permits: No fees or permits required

Schedule: Sunrise to sunset

Maps: Lick Creek Preserve; USGS Chatham

Trail contacts: City Water, Light and Power, Property Management Center, 200 East Lake Shore Drive, Springfield, IL 62712; (217) 757-8660; www.cwlp.com

Finding the trailhead: From exit 93 on I-72 southwest of downtown, take Veterans Parkway, IL 4, south for 1.5 miles to a traffic light and Woodside Road. (The right turn for here will be Spaulding Orchard.) Turn left and follow Woodside Road for 0.4 mile to Old Chatham Road. Turn right on Old Chatham Road and follow it for 0.4 mile to a dead end near the bridge over Lick Creek. The trailhead is located near a small power station. A trailhead kiosk and picnic table are located here. GPS Trailhead Coordinates: N39° 42.977' / W89° 42.116'

The Hike

City Water, Light and Power is the entity that provides water and electricity for greater Springfield. Lake Springfield is its base of operations. The lake is used to store water for public consumption and also to provide water for a power plant. The 57-mile shoreline along the lake is managed by City Water, Light and Power. Lake Springfield is dotted with over eight parks and many residential areas. In its uppermost western reaches lies the seemingly forgotten Lick Creek Preserve. This 340-acre tract encircles the uppermost portion of the Lick Creek embayment. You access it by a dead-end road that was once the primary connector between Chatham and Springfield, Old Chatham Road. IL 4 has replaced Old Chatham Road. Start your hike by tracing this now grown-over road into lush woods on the West Lick Creek Trail. This primitive singletrack footpath leaves the old roadbed and wanders through the bottomlands along Lick Creek and over some hills that rise from the bottomland. Along the way you will see some sizable oaks that were standing a long time back. The trail dead ends at a tributary of Lick Creek, though user-created trails extend beyond the boundaries of Lick Creek Preserve.

After backtracking to the trailhead, you will then join the East Lick Creek Trail. It rolls through bottoms and hills in deep woods and emerges near the shoreline of Lake Springfield. Gain some good views of the lake. The trail continues and meets the Interurban Trail, which connects Springfield and Chatham. This is also the end of the Lick Creek Preserve, which encompasses streams, marshes, and woodlands, providing a home for aquatic and land wildlife in the ever-shrinking natural area and farmland dividing Chatham and Springfield.

On weekends you may be sharing the preserve with mountain bikers. But truthfully, this trail system is underutilized and actually needs more visitation to help keep the trails up. Lick Creek Preserve was established in 1991, but the trails came later. The preserve can be good for spring wildflowers, including Solomon seal, blue cohosh, and mayapple. The variety of hardwoods in this forest will also make it a good fall color hike. Watch for more big trees, especially white oaks. Enjoy the shoreline of Lake Springfield, where waterfowl may be sighted. If you want to extend your walk, head south for the bridge over Lake Springfield on the Interurban Trail.

Miles and Directions

0.0 To pick up the West Lick Creek Trail, pass around a pole gate then continue forward on Old Chatham Road, bridging Lick Creek. The trail follows the roadbed a short way, and then slips left into lush woods. Sugar maple, white oak, cherry, and a thick understory of stinging nettle color the forest green. Open marsh is visible through the trees.

0.3 Step over a streambed.

0.4 Climb a steep hill near IL 4, and then descend into bottomland. You may see deer here.

0.7 Cruise past a huge old-growth white oak. Watch for a second big tree ahead.

0.8 The official trail dead ends near a tributary of Lick Creek. You will see a sign across the Creek indicating the trail is closed beyond this point, as well as a golf course. A user-created trail continues to the right, passing near some houses. Backtrack.

1.6 Return to the trailhead after backtracking on the West Lick Creek Trail. Now walk toward the power station and a large

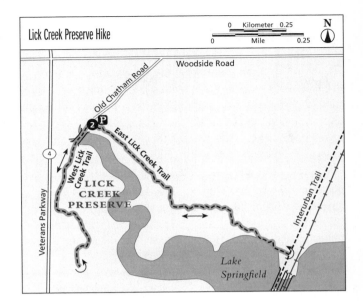

Lick Creek Preserve Hike

0   Kilometer   0.25

0   Mile   0.25

N

Woodside Road

Old Chatham Road

2 P

East Lick Creek Trail

West Lick Creek Trail

4

LICK CREEK PRESERVE

Veterans Parkway

Interurban Trail

Lake Springfield

gate to pick up the East Lick Creek Trail. This path starts on the north side of the small power station and travels east beyond the gate into thick woods. Lake Springfield is visible beyond the trees.

1.7 Cross a wet-weather drainage, and then surmount a hill.

2.1 Pass a property corner post. Curve left.

2.2 Span a small creek on a footbridge.

2.4 Come near the shore of Lake Springfield and then turn away, working over a few more hills.

2.6 Reach the shoreline again. Look for the restored railroad bridge of the Interurban Trail crossing Lake Springfield.

2.7 Meet the Interurban Trail just after passing through a power line clearing. The Interurban Trail leads left to Springfield and right to Chatham. Backtrack.

3.8 Return to the trailhead, completing the hike.

3 Wabash Trail

This popular urban trail traces an old railroad grade through the southwest side of Springfield. The trek starts in a commercial part of the city, and then passes through a residential area. The level grade makes for pleasant walking. You will enjoy this trail with joggers and bicyclers getting their daily exercise.

Distance: 4.2-mile out-and-back
Approximate hiking time: 2.0 to 2.5 hours
Difficulty: Moderate, due to distance only
Trail surface: Asphalt
Best season: Year-round
Other trail users: Joggers, bicyclists
Canine compatibility: Leashed dogs permitted

Fees and permits: No fees or permits required
Schedule: Sunrise to sunset
Maps: Wabash Trail; USGS Springfield West
Trail contacts: Springfield Park District, 2500 South Eleventh Street, Springfield, IL 62703, (217) 544-1751, www.springfieldparks.org

Finding the trailhead: From exit 93 on I-72 south of downtown, take Macarthur Boulevard North for 1.5 miles to Wabash Avenue. Turn left on Wabash Avenue and follow it 0.3 mile to a short connector for Park Street. Turn left on the connector, make a quick right on Park Street, and the trailhead is on your left. GPS Trailhead Coordinates: N39° 45.827' / W89° 40.499'

The Hike

The Wabash Trail and the Interurban Trail can both be accessed from this trailhead. The Interurban Trail leads east then curves south along Macarthur Boulevard, aiming for Lake Springfield and the village of Chatham. The asphalt Wabash Trail stretches 10 feet wide and is slightly elevated. Since this is a linear park, private businesses and houses back to the trail corridor. However, this doesn't detract from the scenery. Trees and other greenery border the track and offer up shade in places, especially near the businesses. In June the mulberry trees will be bearing fruit. Walkers and joggers will be stopping beneath the limbs of the trees, picking the purple fruit. Even if you can't identify a mulberry tree, the dark stain on the trail below them will give their presence away. You will also find tasty blackberries in season.

Rabbits seem to love the trail as well. You will see them hopping about or being still, imagining that you don't see them. They love the grassy areas and brush for a nearby escape. Bird life is also abundant in this green corridor. Come to the first bridge along the trail as it is spans Chatham Road. The trailside scenery becomes more residential and many homeowners have spruced up their adjacent yards for Wabash Trail users. You will see butterfly gardens, landscaping, and other enhancements facing toward the trail. Very few of them have a simple privacy fence. This section of trail also backs up to wooded Washington Park, but you can't access Washington Park at this time, unless you walk off the trail and through neighborhoods.

The trail passes Vredenburgh Park, an 8.5-acre green space added to the Springfield park system in 1974. The park, located off Crusaders Road, is an alternate access for the Wabash Trail. You will pass the parking lot on your right. A large grassy area is complemented with a basketball court, playground, and ball diamond. After bridging busy Veterans Parkway, the trail again enters a commercial area. It currently

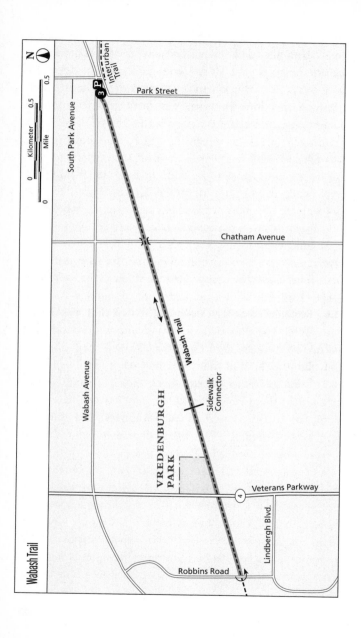

Wabash Trail

N

Interurban Trail

3 P

Park Street

South Park Avenue

0.5   Kilometer   0.5
0   Mile

0

Chatham Avenue

Wabash Avenue

Wabash Trail

Sidewalk Connector

VREDENBURGH PARK

Veterans Parkway

4

Lindbergh Blvd.

Robbins Road

ends at Robbins Road. There is no public trail parking here. The Wabash Rail line once continued west across Illinois and beyond to Kansas City, Missouri. Its eastern terminus was Detroit, Michigan. The line crossed the Wabash River in Indiana and from that derived its name. Allow time and energy to backtrack to the trailhead.

Miles and Directions

0.0 Pick up the Wabash Trail as it travels southwesterly, leaving the commercial district along Wabash Avenue.

0.7 Travel over Chatham Avenue on an iron bridge. The Wabash Trail continues a southwesterly direction in a residential area.

1.4 A sidewalk connects adjoining neighborhoods north and south of the trail, at Idlewild Drive to the south and Saxon Drive to the north.

1.6 Reach the access from Vredenburgh Park. It offers alternate parking as well.

1.7 Cross Veterans Parkway, IL 4, on a high bridge.

2.1 The trail ends at Robbins Road. Backtrack.

4.2 Reach the trailhead, completing the hike.

4 Lost Bridge Trail

This paved path starts at Illinois Department of Transportation headquarters, circles by a pretty lake, and then joins an old railroad grade heading southeast. You will be hiking with IDOT employees at first. The path travels in thick forest, bridging Sugar Creek. The hike keeps on to a tunnel under Hill Top Road. This is a good place to begin backtracking, but the trail continues to Rochester.

Distance: 4.0-mile out-and-back
Approximate hiking time: 2.0 to 2.5 hours
Difficulty: Moderate, due to distance only
Trail surface: Asphalt
Best season: Year-round
Other trail users: Joggers, bicyclists, IDOT employees
Canine compatibility: Leashed dogs permitted

Fees and permits: No fees or permits required
Schedule: Sunrise to sunset
Maps: Lost Bridge Trail; USGS Springfield East
Trail contacts: Springfield Park District, 2500 South Eleventh Street, Springfield, IL 62703; (217) 544-1751; www.springfieldparks.org

Finding the trailhead: From exit 96B on I-72 east of downtown, take South Grand Avenue west for 0.3 mile, and then turn left on Dirksen Parkway. Follow Dirksen Parkway for one mile, turn left on Reilly Drive, entering the IDOT complex. Follow the signs for Lost Bridge Trail, ending up in the southeast corner of the complex, where the Lost Bridge Trail begins. There is parking near the trailhead. GPS Trailhead Coordinates: N39° 46.495' / W89° 36.300'

The Hike

The Lost Bridge Trail was the first rail trail established in greater Springfield. It follows the old Baltimore and Ohio Railroad. The path starts at Illinois Department of Transportation headquarters. The Lost Bridge Trail sets an example for alternate means of transportation and recreation utilizing former railroad rights-of-way. Also, the Lost Bridge Trail demonstrates how employees can increase their health and productivity through daily exercise. Lots of IDOT employees leave their sedentary office jobs for a quick stroll down the Lost Bridge Trail, and then come back refreshed and ready to tackle their tasks.

There was a bit of a fight in getting the trail established. It was finally opened in 1995. The name came from the bridge over Sugar Creek, which you will cross, being dismantled by the Baltimore and Ohio Railroad for scrap salvage, rather than being kept for the trail. The bridge was lost and the Illinois Department of Transportation had to build its own bridge over Sugar Creek. Sugar Creek is the outflow stream of Lake Springfield. Since it comes from a dam and lake, Sugar Creek is usually clearer than other streams, including the Sangamon River, into which it flows east of downtown.

After leaving the campus of Illinois Department of Transportation, the Lost Bridge Trail joins the Baltimore and Ohio Railroad. Its course heads due southeast. Trail distances are posted in half mile increments. The woods are very thick here and form a canopy over the trail. This makes it a good summertime hiking option. The lush forest also mutes the noise from the interstate as you pass under it. The trail ends in Rochester after 5 miles. A connector leads to Community Park. Long-term plans are to connect the Lost Bridge Trail

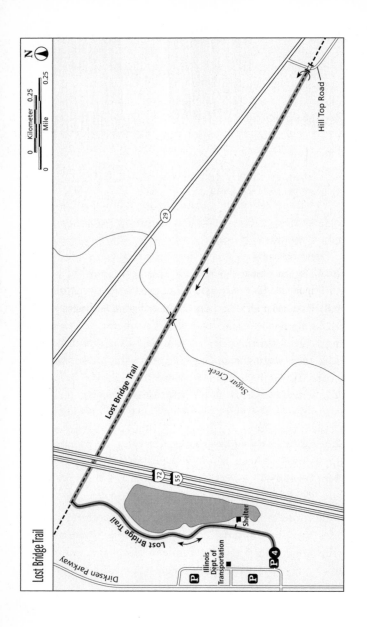

Lost Bridge Trail

with the Lincoln Prairie Trail in Taylorville. This particular hike goes to the tunnel below Hill Top Road. This tunnel is nothing special in and of itself, but is simply a good marker at which to turn around.

Miles and Directions

0.0 Leave the southeastern corner of the IDOT facility, joining an asphalt path east through woods. Shortly, reach a hilltop where you can view IDOT headquarters building, the Lost Bridge Trail, and a lake. I-55/72 stands in the background. The lake was created for fill to elevate a nearby interstate interchange. Descend between the building and the lake.

0.1 A spur trail leads right to a covered picnic shelter and a fishing platform.

0.7 The path curves southeast and joins the bed of the Baltimore and Ohio Railroad. The forest canopy here is thick.

0.8 Pass under I-55/72. Keep southeast toward Rochester.

1.1 Cross an IDOT road.

1.2 Cross Sugar Creek on a bridge built for the trail. The old bridge was dismantled and "lost." The woods remain thick along the creek, but fields extend beyond.

1.7 Hills rise beside the trail. The old railroad grade was cut into the land, keeping the line level. This creates an intimate trail environment.

2.0 Reach the Hill Top Road tunnel. A spur trail is located just beyond the tunnel and leads to Hill Top Road. Backtrack.

4.0 Return to Illinois Department of Transportation headquarters and the trailhead, completing the hike.

5 Carpenter Park Hike

One of Springfield's oldest parks and a designated Illinois state nature preserve, Carpenter Park presents rich woodland rising from the banks of the Sangamon River. A series of interconnected trails explores the 434-acre grounds. This particular hike traipses through dense woods and passes a wooded wetland pond. It then heads downslope to the Sangamon River and through floodplain forest. The final part of the trek travels along the slopes above the river and culminates in a sandstone outcrop overlook on the river before returning to the trailhead.

Distance: 2.1-mile loop
Approximate hiking time: 1.0 to 2.0 hours
Difficulty: Moderate
Trail surface: Natural surfaces
Best season: Year-round
Other trail users: None
Canine compatibility: Leashed dogs permitted

Fees and permits: No fees or permits required
Schedule: Sunrise to sunset
Maps: Carpenter Park; USGS Springfield East, Springfield West
Trail contacts: Springfield Park District, 2500 South Eleventh Street, Springfield, IL 62703; (217) 544-1751; www.spring fieldparks.org

Finding the trailhead: From exit 100B on I-55/72 east of downtown, take Sangamon Avenue west for 0.6 mile to Dirksen Parkway. Turn right and follow Dirksen Parkway for 2 miles to Business Loop 55. Turn right on Business Loop 55 and follow it 1.1 miles, crossing the Sangamon River to Cabin Smoke Trail. Turn left on Cabin Smoke Trail, and then, shortly, veer left again into Carpenter Park. Follow the park road to a picnic shelter and the trailhead. GPS Trailhead Coordinates: N39° 52.283' / W89° 37.130'

The Hike

Carpenter Park has been a part of the Springfield Park system since 1922. This land on the north bank of the Sangamon River features a variety of habitats ranging from river bottom and floodplain forest to drier hilltop hardwoods and even some sandstone rock outcrops rising from the river. The park itself is over 400 acres, 322 of which are a designated Illinois state nature preserve. William Carpenter established himself at this location in 1820. He operated a ferry crossing the Sangamon River in addition to farming and running a flour and sawmill powered by the Sangamon. The property stayed in his family until his daughter donated the land to the city of Springfield. Later, the historic and attractive stone picnic shelter you see at the trailhead was erected. Today, a network of singletrack paths winds throughout the woods and provides hikers with an opportunity to explore this nature preserve, rich with birds and mammals that call the Sangamon River valley home.

The footbed is primarily grass or dirt. The interconnected trails can be a little confusing, since there are not only a lot of short interconnected trails but also some user-created paths. That being said, it is almost impossible to get lost as you have the Sangamon River to your south, Business Loop 55 to your east, and Cabin Smoke Trail (and a golf course) to your north. You may get a little bit turned around at some point but don't sweat it.

This loop leaves the historic stone shelter and makes its way to the North Road Trail, a wide track that actually travels east–west. The rest of the trails are narrow footpaths. You begin heading downhill toward the Sangamon River. The area is good deer habitat. After several trail intersections, the River View Trail drops into bottomland hardwoods dominated by silver maple. The trail can be muddy here at times. You will soon saddle alongside the Sangamon River. Enjoy aquatic views culminating in a trip to a sheer sandstone bluff. Here you can look down the river and up close at the thousands of carvings in the soft stone left by visitors. From the bluff it is but a short trip back to the parking area. Numerous user-created paths make your return more difficult than it should be.

Miles and Directions

0.0 As you face the stone picnic shelter, look right and pick up the Twisted Tree Trail. Join a singletrack path wandering northeasterly in woods.

0.2 Cross a wetland on a boardwalk. Ahead, turn right and go just a short distance to meet North Road Trail, a wide path, near a wetland pond. Turn left on the North Road Trail.

0.3 The White Oak Trail leaves left. Keep straight on the North Road Trail.

0.5 Turn left on the singletrack West Woods Trail. North Road Trail keeps straight.

0.6 The Red Bud Trail leaves left back toward the parking area. Keep straight, still on the West Woods Trail.

0.8 At a trail junction, a grassy trail leads right to a field. Stay left, still on the West Woods Trail.

0.9 Come to a trail intersection. Here, the Blackberry Trail keeps straight. However, you veer right joining the River View Trail.

1.1 The Sangamon River comes into view. Begin traveling alongside the watercourse, and then drift back from the river in big oaks, cottonwoods, maples, and sycamores.

1.5 Reach an intersection after climbing a hill. Here, the River View Trail goes left to the parking area, while another trail

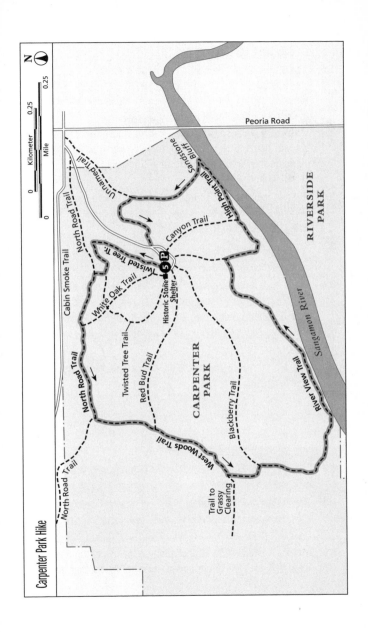

Carpenter Park Hike

N

Kilometer
0   0.25

Mile
0   0.25

Peoria Road

Sandstone Bluff

High Point Trail

Unnamed Trail

North Road Trail

Cabin Smoke Trail

Canyon Trail

Twisted Tree Tr.

White Oak Trail

5 P

Historic Stone Shelter

North Road Trail

Twisted Tree Trail

Red Bud Trail

Blackberry Trail

CARPENTER PARK

River View Trail

Sangamon River

RIVERSIDE PARK

North Road Trail

West Woods Trail

Trail to Grassy Clearing

leads back down to the Sangamon. Stay right and drop steeply back to the river.

1.6 Come to another intersection near the river. Here, the Canyon Trail goes left to the parking area. Keep straight along the river, joining the High Point Trail as bluffs rise and the going gets a little tougher.

1.8 Come to a sheer sandstone bluff rising above the Sangamon. The Business Loop 55 bridge is within sight. Enjoy views downriver. Beyond this point, turn away from the river, climbing on a ridgeline.

2.0 The trail reaches a final major intersection. Here, make a left and cross a wooden bridge over a small creek. The trail going right leads to the park entrance.

2.1 Return to the parking area, completing the hike.

6 New Salem Loop

This hike explores the natural side of New Salem State Historic Site, a reconstructed historic village where Abraham Lincoln lived six formative years. The hike travels through forest along Rocky Branch before dipping to cross IL 97. You then climb steeply up Cardinal Ridge and meander back down to the shore of the Sangamon River. Travel through bottomland and along hills on a section of old Pritchettville Road. The hike crosses back over IL 97 and climbs to the trailhead, which is located at the entrance to the historic village. Consider visiting the village in conjunction with your hike.

Distance: 3.3-mile double loop
Approximate hiking time: 2.0 to 2.5 hours
Difficulty: Moderate, does have hills
Trail surface: Natural surfaces, a little bit of asphalt
Best season: Year-round
Other trail users: None
Canine compatibility: Leashed dogs permitted
Fees and permits: No fees or permits required
Schedule: Nov 1–Feb 28: Open Wed through Sun 8:00 a.m.–4:00 p.m., Mar 1–Apr 15: Open Wed through Sun 9:00 a.m.–5:00 p.m., Apr 16–Sept 15: Open Sun through Sat 9:00 a.m.–5:00 p.m., Sept 16–Oct 31: Open Wed through Sun 9:00 a.m.–5:00 p.m. Call ahead to make sure it is open.
Maps: New Salem Historic Site; USGS Salisbury
Trail contacts: Lincoln's New Salem State Historic Site, 15588 History Lane, Petersburg, IL 62675; (217) 632-4000; www .lincolnnewsalem.com

Finding the trailhead: From the intersection of IL 4 / Veterans Parkway and IL 97 / Jefferson Street, west of downtown, take IL 97 north to a traffic light at the intersection with IL 125. Turn right at the traffic light, staying with IL 97 for 11.5 miles from the light to the entrance to Lincoln's New Salem Road and the historic site entrance. Follow the main road toward the visitor center. At 0.2 mile the main parking area and visitor center will open to your right. You, however, keep forward just a short distance, and then look left for the Mentor Graham's Footsteps Trail on the left-hand side of the parking area, away from the visitor center. GPS Trailhead Coordinates: N39° 58.655' / W89° 50.872'

The Hike

It is said that Abraham Lincoln found his direction in life while living at New Salem, Illinois. Thanks to the effort of private citizens and the state, New Salem and the period of time relating to Abraham Lincoln have been reconstructed so that you can enjoy this living history as well as the natural area around it. New Salem was a thriving community for less than eight years when it fell into decline as a result of nearby Petersburg being named the county seat.

Private citizens have been working to keep New Salem a reconstructed village for over a century. The state of Illinois joined the effort in 1919, and then in 1930 the place really took off with the addition of historic buildings and the reconstruction of period buildings of Lincoln's time at New Salem.

Today you can enjoy not only the buildings of that time, but also the furnishings, décor, and lifeways of the nineteenth century. You can also learn about the actual residents of New Salem, the jobs they had, and their interactions with their fellow citizens, especially Abraham

Lincoln. If you're here during the summer time, enjoy live productions based on Lincoln's life at New Salem. The park also features a large picnic ground and campground, as well as a museum store, visitor center, and refreshment and souvenir shop.

But don't forget about the hike. Most visitors do. You first join the Mentor Graham's Footsteps Trail. This interpretive path travels through woodland, where you can identify trees and some historic sites along the way. The path crosses over Rocky Branch, a pretty tributary of the Sangamon River. Beyond the interpretive trail, heavily wooded Cardinal Ridge leads to uplands and the Shady Hollow Trail. That path crisscrosses Pritchettville Road before dropping to the Sangamon River. In places the hike follows the old crumbling and abandoned lower Pritchettville Road. Thousands of silver maples will lie between you and the river. The final part of the hike climbs back along Rocky Branch watershed. Almost the entire trek travels through rich hardwoods, making it a favorable early fall destination. Since it also travels moist hollows along the riverbed, you will be able to see spring wildflowers as well.

Miles and Directions

0.0 Pick up the Mentor Graham's Footsteps Trail on the south end of the main parking lot. Enter lush woods, descending on wood and earth steps.

0.2 Split right at the trail junction. Descend to cross a tributary of Rocky Branch, itself, rocky and clear. Climb a hill.

0.4 Stay right at a trail junction. The trail leading left shortcuts the loop. Continue downhill toward Rocky Branch.

0.5 Bridge Rocky Branch just after passing the other end of the Mentor Graham's Footsteps Trail. Open onto the

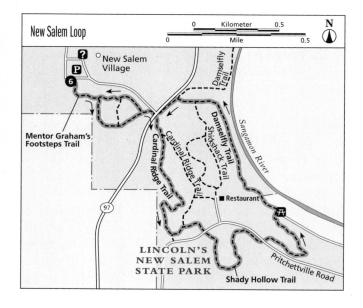

park entrance road, and then carefully cross IL 97. Look right across a grassy field for the signposts indicating the entrance to the Cardinal Ridge Trail at the edge of the woods. Begin climbing steeply up Cardinal Ridge. Stout hardwoods shade the path.

1.1 After leveling off, reach a trail junction. A short trail leaves right to Pritchettville Road. Stay left, still in woods.

1.2 Stay right, as the trail leading left, Cardinal Ridge Trail, heads back toward IL 97. Soon cross Pritchettville Road and join the Shady Hollow Trail.

1.8 Cross Pritchettville Road again after coming alongside it for a while. Begin descending toward the Sangamon River.

2.2 Come to a picnic area above the Sangamon River. Restrooms and water are nearby. Leave left, joining the Damselfly Trail on a crumbling asphalt path that was once the

continuation of Pritchettville Road. Leave the pavement.
View the river below.

2.8 Pass the Shickshack Trail on your left after leaving the
Sangamon River. Ahead, reach IL 97, and then turn left,
following 97 and returning to the entrance road. Pick up the
Mentor Graham's Footsteps Trail, this time staying right, on
new trail.

3.2 Complete the second loop after passing the shortcut. Continue uphill on wood and earth steps, now backtracking.

3.3 Return to the main parking area, completing the double loop
hike.

7 Gridley Lake Loop

This loop trail was specifically designed for foot travel only. You will start at the boat ramp on Gridley Lake, and then span a little bridge. From there you will work around the many arms and fingers of the impoundment. This area is managed for scenic value and wildlife. I have seen deer on this trail, including a fawn. While mimicking the shoreline, the path travels up and down over low hills in a mix of prairie and forest. The scenery and views just keep changing. You will also see anglers boating on the lake and fishermen using a designated platform.

Distance: 2.9-mile out-and-back
Approximate hiking time: 1.5 to 2.0 hours
Difficulty: Moderate
Trail surface: Grass
Best season: Spring through fall
Other trail users: None
Canine compatibility: Leashed dogs permitted
Fees and permits: No fees or permits required

Schedule: Sunrise to sunset, trails closed Nov 1 to Apr 15
Maps: Jim Edgar Panther Creek State Fish and Wildlife Area; USGS Ashland
Trail contacts: 10149 County Highway 11, Chandlerville, IL 62627; (217) 452-7741; www .dnr.illinois.gov

Finding the trailhead: From the intersection of IL 4 / Veterans Parkway and IL 97 / Jefferson Street, west of downtown, take IL 97 north to a traffic light. At this light, keep straight, joining IL 125. Travel for a total of 19.6 miles from Veterans Parkway to Newmansville Road. Turn right on Newmansville Road and follow it 4.2 miles to Gridley Road. Turn left on Gridley Road and follow it 1.4 miles to the left turn into Gridley Lake Picnic and Boat Access Area. GPS Trailhead Coordinates: N39° 57.3345' / W90° 4.3623'

The Hike

Jim Edgar Panther Creek State Fish and Wildlife Area averages over 700,000 visitors per year. These visitors come in all stripes. They aren't just your average hunters and fishermen. Nature lovers of all kinds come here, including us hikers, but also campers, equestrians, and mountain bikers. Bird enthusiasts visit the park also. Thankfully, the managers at the park have developed destinations and facilities for all types of users. The Gridley Lake Trail is for foot travel only and thus designates a specific path for those who want the quiet and solitude brought about by hiking. Foot travel can include jogging, trail running, and nature study, not merely hiking. You will likely see all the above if you do this path enough times. The lake also provides opportunities for anglers with its fishing platform for those without a boat.

The lake backs up a nameless tributary of Panther Creek. Willows drape over the water along much of the shoreline. The lake has standing and dead snags as well as water grasses, in addition to open water surface. Amphibians claim their place along the shore. Cattails rise from the shallows. Note the wood duck boxes planted on posts above the lake. Small cleared areas allow direct access to the lake for scenic viewing and for fishing. The path meanders into woods, which offer a cool and dark alternative to the open prairie hiking. But the hike as a whole is under or beside trees most of the way, with some open sections. You are never far from the water and most often can view it through the trees at the very least. Hardwoods such as oak and hickory proliferate in the woods, along with locust and hackberry. Hilly terrain adds vertical variety to the trek.

Make your way around one arm of the lake, then another, and then you briefly come out on a road before resuming your meanderings. The trail often takes you just feet across from where you were earlier as it snakes around the embayments. If you have any navigational doubts, just stay to the right everywhere, keeping as close as possible to the lake.

Miles and Directions

0.0 As you face the Gridley Lake boat ramp, leave left from the parking area and in a short time span a foot bridge dividing the main lake from a small wetland. Beyond the bridge, follow a mown path along the lakeshore.

0.1 Meet another mown path that also comes from the boat ramp. Continue along the willow-studded shoreline.

0.5 Stay right along the lakeshore as a mown path leads left toward cropland and Gridley Road. The foot-only trail continues straddling field and forest as it curves back in a westerly direction around the first major arm of the lake.

0.8 You can see the trailhead from here but the trail takes you in an easterly direction up the longest arm of Gridley Lake.

1.2 Reach Degroot Lane. Turn right and briefly follow the gravel road, and then turn right again and rejoin the grassy trail back along the shore of Gridley Lake.

1.5 Stay right on a wider mown path, an access road, crossing an earthen dam that backs up a small pond. After crossing the dam, stay right, resuming your hike on a narrower grassy track bordering the impoundment. A shortcut keeps straight.

1.8 Reach the other end of the shortcut and stay right, still curving along the lakeshore.

2.1 You are so close to the trailhead, you could swim across the lake to reach it. Continue hiking in field and woods.

Gridley Lake Loop

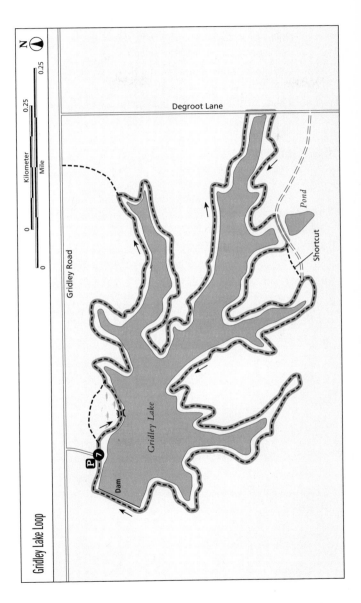

N

Kilometer
0   0.25

Mile
0   0.25

Degroot Lane

Gridley Road

Gridley Lake

Dam

P 7

Pond

Shortcut

2.2 Come to another point looking out on the trailhead. Continue circling around the southwest side of Gridley Lake, working around the last big lake arm.

2.8 Come to the dam of Gridley Lake. Here, turn right heading north and curve right at the far end of the dam.

2.9 Return to the trailhead and boat ramp, completing the hike.

8 Prairie Lake Hike

This hike at Jim Edgar Panther Creek State Fish and Wildlife Area travels around alluring Prairie Lake. True to its name, the impoundment is bordered by wood and meadow. The Lakeside Trail leaves the lake dam and circles around a many-fingered embayment, where you will enjoy multiple aquatic perspectives and many hills. Views also extend on the rolling prairie. Reach the head of the embayment, and then turn around at a point near the lake. The entire Lakeside Trail stretches 17 miles around Prairie Lake, if you are feeling really ambitious.

Distance: 3.8-mile out-and-back

Approximate hiking time: 2.0 to 2.5 hours

Difficulty: Moderate

Trail surface: Mostly grass

Best season: Spring through fall

Other trail users: Mountain bicyclers

Canine compatibility: Leashed dogs permitted

Fees and permits: No fees or permits required

Schedule: Sunrise to sunset, trails closed from Nov 1 to Apr 15

Maps: Lakeside Trail; USGS Ashland

Trail contacts: 10149 County Highway 11, Chandlerville, IL 62627; (217) 452-7741; www .dnr.illinois.gov

Finding the trailhead: From the intersection of IL 4 / Veterans Parkway and IL 97 / Jefferson Street, west of downtown, take IL 97 north to a traffic light. At this light, keep straight, joining IL 125. Travel for a total of 19.6 miles from Veterans Parkway to Newmansville Road. Turn right on Newmansville Road and follow it 7 miles to the state park entrance and CR 11. Turn left onto the CR 11 and follow it 1.2 miles to the left turn into Prairie Lake. Turn left toward Prairie Lake and go just a short distance, and then turn left toward the boat ramp. Park near the boat ramp. Pick up the lakeside trail in the eastern corner of the parking area, following a grassy track toward the lake dam. GPS Trailhead Coordinates: N39° 59.764' / W90° 3.646'

The Hike

Large wild areas are hard to come by in Illinois, but Jim Edgar Panther Creek State Fish and Wildlife Area is an exception. The state park was purchased from Commonwealth Edison Company in 1993. The company was planning to build a power plant here, but it didn't happen. Instead, we have over 16,000 acres of hills, bottomlands, forests, lakes, prairies, and farmland. This adds up to a large contiguous area for recreation such as hiking, boating, camping, hunting, and fishing. As a matter of fact, this is the largest fish and wildlife area in the state. It has a total of 73 miles of trails for the outdoor enthusiast. All of them are open to hikers, though they share some of them with mountain bikers, such as on this hike, and in other places, equestrians. However, with this much trail mileage in one state park, there's plenty of room to spread out. This particular hike traverses a scenic section of the Lakeside Trail, which snakes its way 17 miles around Prairie Lake. It follows the shoreline, curving around embayments and coves, while rolling through woods and prairies. These prairies are being restored with native grasses. The wildflower displays in summer can be impressive.

First cross the dam, which offers unobstructed views of Prairie Lake. The trail then curves up a more intimate embayment that gets ever smaller. Smaller coves, offshoots of these already small embayments, are often filled with fallen timber upon which turtles lie. Bullfrogs will be croaking. Standing snags attract birds. Other wildlife are attracted to not only the water, but the edges of water and land, as well as the edges between forest and prairie. To top it off the area is managed for wildlife. Thus, your chances of seeing a deer or other critter are pretty good, especially if you come during morning or evening.

The trail most often travels the nexus between prairie and woodland. Trees border most of the lake, and you will see the water through the forest or between a scattered tree or two when the trail comes really close to the shoreline. Locust, walnut, cottonwood, and oak rise in the forest. Sumac grows in sunny areas. In open areas you can see the swales in the prairie. There's no spectacular view at the end of the hike, just a place to turn around and return to the trailhead, looking a second time for highlights you may have missed before.

Miles and Directions

0.0 As you face the Prairie Lake boat ramp, hike to the left from the parking area on a grassy track; in a short time you will cross Prairie Lake dam. Lake views open atop the riprap-bordered impoundment, as well as views of the lands below the dam.

0.2 Drop off the dam to cross the dam spillway, overgrown with grasses.

0.4 The Lakeside Trail enters woods. From here on out the trail drifts in and out of forest or directly alongside trees with just a few excursions into the open prairie.

1.1 Return to the main embayment after circling a couple of coves. Soon bisect thick woods.

1.4 Reach the upper end of the embayment you have been following. Here, the path climbs a grassy hill before curving back toward the lake.

1.9 After coming near a wildlife food plot, the trail curves back toward the lake and reaches a wooded narrow ridge. The

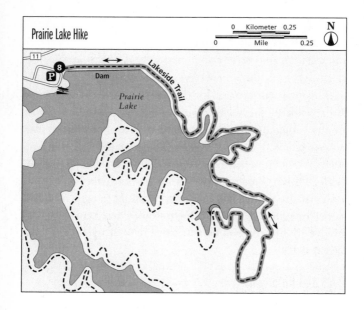

lake is in sight through the trees but not too close. This is a good place to turn around unless you want to tackle 15 more miles around the lake.

3.8 Return to the trailhead, completing the hike.

⑨ Drake Lake Sampler

This loop makes a circuit near the least visited of the three lakes at Jim Edgar Panther Creek State Fish and Wildlife Area. It leaves the parking area to bisect its dam, and then rambles through thick woods to the far shore. Hikers then backtrack to the dam and drop into hilly terrain, crossing a deep valley before looping back to the trailhead. The defined distance of this hike is short, but the Drake Lake Trail makes a four-plus-mile loop around the lake; additional trails are available, including a connector to Prairie Lake and its Lakeside Trail. A complete park trail map is available at the park office, which you pass on the way in.

Distance: 1.6-mile balloon loop
Approximate hiking time: 1.0 hour
Difficulty: Easy
Trail surface: Grass
Best season: Spring through fall
Other trail users: Mountain bicyclers
Canine compatibility: Leashed dogs permitted

Fees and permits: No fees or permits required
Schedule: Sunrise to sunset, trails closed from Nov 1 to Apr 15
Maps: Jim Edgar Panther Creek State Fish and Wildlife Area; USGS Newmansville
Trail contacts: 10149 County Highway 11, Chandlerville, IL 62627; (217) 452-7741; www.dnr.illinois.gov

Finding the trailhead: From the intersection of IL 4 / Veterans Parkway and IL 97 / Jefferson Street, west of downtown, take IL 97 north to a traffic light. At this light, keep straight, joining IL 125. Travel for a total of 19.6 miles from Veterans Parkway to Newmansville Road. Turn right on Newmansville Road and follow it 7 miles to the state park entrance and CR 11. Turn left onto CR 11 and stay straight, now on Creek Road, as CR 11 veers left at the park office. Follow CR 11 / Creek Road for a total of 2.4 miles from Newmansville Road. Turn right on Gurney Road and follow it 0.7 mile to dead end at the Drake Lake boat ramp and trailhead, which has restrooms and a picnic shelter. GPS Trailhead Coordinates: N40° 0.2519' / W90° 5.0848'

The Hike

Drake Lake is located in the heart of the Jim Edgar Panther Creek State Fish and Wildlife Area. This impoundment is encircled by a loop trail that traces its shoreline. This includes traveling up the narrow arms of the lake as well as the main body, over hills, through thick woods, and also in prairie environment. Most lakes you'll visit have houses or other developments on them. This lake is bordered by nothing but forest and that is why whether you are hiking, paddling, or fishing, Drake Lake is an eye-pleasing destination. The Jim Edgar Panther Creek State Fish and Wildlife Area is managed by the Illinois Department of Natural Resources. It makes sense that they would maintain such a natural scenic impoundment as Drake Lake. Their mission is to "protect, enhance and manage" the state's natural and cultural resources. This specifically means that they manage the state's wildlife and fisheries. In doing so, they also manage the environment for non-game flora and fauna, from muskrats to butterflies. They recognize that you can't manage one specific strand in the web of life without addressing all the other adjacent strands as well. Much of their work is funded by those who purchase sporting licenses to fish and hunt at places such as Jim Edgar Panther Creek State Fish and Wildlife Area. The law requires that these fees go back into wildlife and fish restoration. So whether you see a buck darting away in the forest, or a fish jumping in Drake Lake, or a restored prairie through which you walk, the Illinois Department of Natural Resources has likely improved the habitat for the life that lives within this preserve.

It is not out of the question that you will see all of the above on this hike. The trek starts at the boat ramp, where anglers may be loading or unloading. It then travels alongside the shoreline, where you may see fish jumping or waterfowl. Anglers will be casting for catfish, bream, and largemouth bass. The hike then spans the Drake Lake dam and wanders the far, heavily wooded shoreline. A hardwood forest rife with hickory and oak cloaks the edge of the lake. If you want to extend your distance, this is a good trail section to do it on. Simply continue walking around the lake and turn back at your leisure. The final stretch of the hike travels through some open land before descending a steep hill and walking the bottoms below the dam. Here you will see a connector to Prairie Lake, but that may add on more miles than you want. Finally, after dipping into the bottom-land, you will make one of the steeper climbs in this guide back to the dam. From here is but a short walk to the boat ramp and trailhead.

Miles and Directions

0.0 As you face Drake Lake, walk left from the parking area on a grassy track along the park shore. Shortly, you will come to a grassy point used by bank anglers. Continue along the shoreline.

0.1 Join an auto-width mown path that has also come from the parking area. This is used by park personnel to access areas on the far side of the Drake Lake dam.

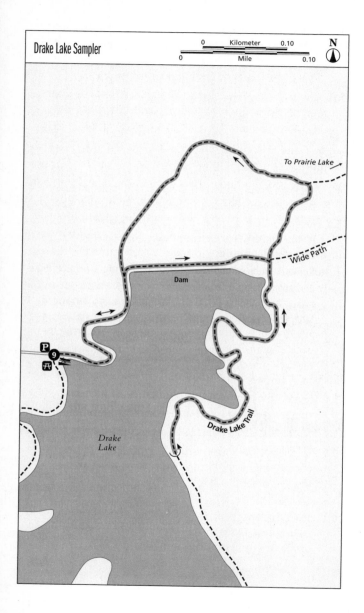

0.2 Reach Drake Lake dam. The wide mown path crosses the dam, while a narrower grassy trail goes left. This is your return route. For now cross the dam, soaking in views of Drake Lake. The trail climbs a hill beyond the dam.

0.3 Come to a four-way junction. Turn right on the narrow mown path, which enters woodland and begins to circle the eastern shore of Drake Lake. Locust trees are giving way to more shade-tolerant hardwoods.

0.7 You are directly across from the boat ramp in a stand of hickory trees. Continue just a short distance until reaching the longest arm of the lake. This is a good place to backtrack; however, you can also extend your hike at this point.

1.1 Return to the four-way junction. This time keep straight, northbound on a slender mown path. The wide grassy access road leaves right.

1.2 Come to another intersection. Here, a spur trail leads right and connects to Prairie Lake. This is another chance to extend your hike, but remember to build in ample return time. Otherwise, turn left here on a trail marked with a snowmobile sign. Begin descending to the bottomland below the dam. Step over the unnamed tributary of Cox Creek that Drake Lake backs up. This crossing should be easy, and the creek may even be dry.

1.4 Reach the dam after surmounting a steep grassy hill. Begin backtracking toward the boat ramp and trailhead.

1.6 Complete the hike after returning to the boat ramp and trailhead.

10 Governors Trail

Rewarding hilltop views in Central Illinois? Yes, sir. This hike will take you to two of them. Start down low in the Panther Creek Valley and make a likely wet ford of Panther Creek. The trail enters a steep walled hollow deeply shrouded in hardwoods. It then crosses the stream that makes the hollow before climbing to an open, grassy, upland prairie. Here, you follow a spur trail to an overlook high above Panther Creek. The second part of the hike drops back to bottomland and makes a second climb to another viewpoint. This one has a contemplation bench. Enjoy the views from here before returning to the trailhead. The downside is that you will be sharing the trail with equestrians and some trail sections may be muddy.

Distance: 2.5-mile balloon loop with spurs
Approximate hiking time: 2.0 hours
Difficulty: More challenging due to hill climbs and a stream ford
Trail surface: Natural surfaces
Best season: Spring through fall
Other trail users: Equestrians, a few mountain bikers
Canine compatibility: Leashed dogs permitted

Fees and permits: No fees or permits required
Schedule: Sunrise to sunset, trails closed from Nov 1 to Apr 15
Maps: Governors Trail; USGS Newmansville
Trail contacts: Jim Edgar Panther Creek State Fish and Wildlife Area, 10149 County Highway 11, Chandlerville, IL 62627; (217) 452-7741; www.dnr.illinois.gov

Finding the trailhead: From the intersection of IL 4 / Veterans Parkway and IL 97 / Jefferson Street, west of downtown, take IL 97 north to a traffic light. At this light, keep straight, joining IL 125.

Travel for a total of 19.6 miles from Veterans Parkway to Newmans-ville Road. Turn right on Newmansville Road and follow it 7 miles to the state park entrance and CR 11. Turn left onto CR 11 and stay straight, now on Creek Road, as CR 11 veers left at the park office. Follow CR 11/Creek Road for a total of 6.8 miles from Newmansville Road. Turn left into parking area Q-4 on your left, just before Creek Road bridges Cox Creek. GPS Trailhead Coordinates: N40° 1.394' / W90° 6.894'

The Hike

The Panther Creek Valley is laced with hills cloaked in a mix of forest and prairie. And to make things better, this valley is located within the protected confines of the Jim Edgar Pan-ther Creek State Fish and Wildlife Area. Therefore, Panther Creek Valley offers a stark contrast to the flat farmlands of Central Illinois and a great opportunity for hiking. The Gov-ernors Trail presents 26 miles of hiking divided into three distinct yet connected loops of 9, 11, and 6 miles. Fourteen scenic overlooks are scattered throughout this trail system. You will visit two of them. The hiking is very rewarding, but if you can't stand walking trails that horses tread then read no further. However, I think the upside of the hills, views, and attractive stream that is Panther Creek outweigh the negatives of occasional muddy spots and horse manure.

Be aware that your hike starts with a challenge before you even get to the hills. First you must cross Panther Creek. There is no bridge here and unless it is late in the summer or early fall, you will have to get your feet wet. In spring the water may be excessively high, but most likely it will be flowing moderately and about shin deep. This still requires wetting your feet, and remember that once you cross the stream and do your hike, you'll have to cross it a second time to complete the trek. I have simply taken off my shoes and socks, and then walked across barefoot. But the ford is close enough to the trailhead that you could bring some flip-flops to cross the stream, hide them in the woods, execute your hike, and then return to cross a second time with your flip-flops or water shoes.

Beyond the ford you will begin to enjoy the hilly scenery as you clamber up a steeply wooded hollow cut by a clear streamlet. After the trail opens onto uplands, you reach the first viewpoint. This looks across the Panther Creek Valley at an auto-accessible overlook known as Jake's Point. The hike will then take you back down to grassy bottomland along Panther Creek, only to return up another steep hill and a second view. The second one is my favorite, as it is in open meadow and allows farther views across the valley. It also has a contemplation bench for relaxing. Your return trip makes a short cut, and before you know it, you'll be back at the ford again and have completed your hike.

Miles and Directions

0.0 Standing at the trailhead, kiosk trails go left and right—go left. Walk just a short distance, and then you come to yet another trail split. Turn right here and reach the rocky ford of Panther Creek. Travel in mixed woodland of walnut and prairie grasses.

0.2 Cross a clear stream, and then enter a steeply wooded hollow.

0.4 Make a second crossing of the stream and continue climbing.

0.7 Top out in prairie and reach a trail junction. Stay left, entering a strip of woods.

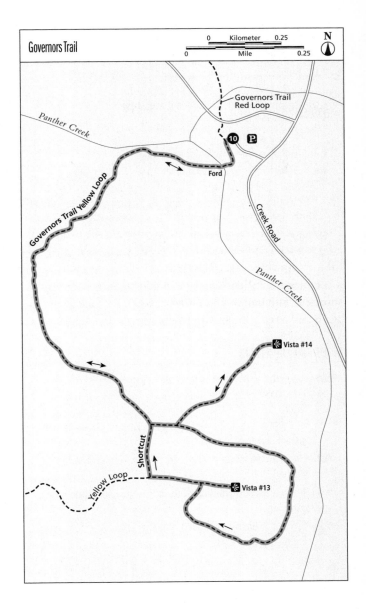

Governors Trail

0   Kilometer   0.25
0   Mile   0.25

N

Governors Trail
Red Loop

Panther Creek

10 P

Ford

Creek Road

Panther Creek

Governors Trail Yellow Loop

Vista #14

Shortcut

Yellow Loop

Vista #13

0.8 Come to a second junction after emerging from the wooded strip. Take the spur leading left to Vista #14. Walk a ridgeline mixed with woods and field.

1.0 Reach Vista #14. Views of Jakes Point and the Panther Creek Valley open. Backtrack.

1.2 Return to main loop. Stay left and descend toward Panther Creek. Come to the valley floor and turn right, upstream, in clumpy grasses.

1.4 Turn up a side hollow and climb.

1.6 Come to the spur to Vista #13. Turn right and make the short walk to the vista. Excellent views open from the meadow. Jakes Point is visible. Backtrack, and then resume the main loop.

1.7 Turn right on a grassy mown shortcut trail as the main Yellow Loop keeps straight. The shortcut travels north along the edge of wood and meadow.

1.8 Make a trail junction. You were here before. Keep straight and backtrack toward Panther Creek.

2.5 Complete the hike after making a second ford of Panther Creek.

11 Salt Creek Trail

This trail at Edward R. Madigan State Park travels bottom-land along scenic Salt Creek. Leave the Salt Creek Canoe Launch North, and then travel upstream under a canopy of tall silver maples, ash, and cottonwood. Trailside bluffs allow for stream vantage points. Hike along the waterway to reach a picnic area. Here, you can backtrack or make a loop. Several trail intersections can make the circuit a little more complicated than necessary, but a little mental navigation and the directions provided will get you back to the trailhead.

Distance: 1.9-mile loop
Approximate hiking time: 1.0 hour
Difficulty: Easy, multiple inter-sections can be confusing
Trail surface: Natural surfaces
Best season: Year-round
Other trail users: None
Canine compatibility: Leashed dogs permitted

Fees and permits: No fees or permits required
Schedule: Sunrise to sunset
Maps: Salt Creek Trail; USGS Lincoln West, Broadwell
Trail contacts: Edward R. Madi-gan State Park, 1366 1010th Avenue, Lincoln, IL 62656; (217)732-1552; www.dnr.illinois .gov

Finding the trailhead: From exit 123 on I-55, north of downtown and south of the town of Lincoln, take Business Loop 55 North for 0.6 mile. Turn right at the entrance sign for Edward R. Madigan State Park. Cross the railroad tracks, and then stay left, entering the park. Follow the signs for the fishing and boat ramp. You will end up at the Salt Creek Canoe Launch North. GPS Trailhead Coordinates: N40° 7.507' / W89° 23.255'

The Hike

Formerly named Rail Splitter State Park, this 974-acre preserve has been in public hands for a while. It was transferred to the state parks in 1970 from the Illinois Department of Mental Health. Even to this day, it has non-park uses—a prison occupies adjacent land. But no worries—if the park were unsafe, people wouldn't be allowed to come here. In actuality, your biggest danger will be getting confused at the numerous trails that comprise the greater Salt Creek Trail. It is laid out with multiple junctions in the bottomlands of the Salt Creek Valley. Even so, just a little common sense will keep you apprised of your position. Additionally, the trail is hemmed in on two sides by Salt Creek, and the other two sides by park roads, so unless you jump in Salt Creek and swim across to the other side, you won't be truly lost for long. Here are a few tips for not getting lost: Stay left at every trail junction, keeping Salt Creek to your left. If you do this, you'll end up without fail at a picnic area where the North Park Access Road ends. Then you can simply backtrack 0.9 mile to the trailhead.

You will see visitors angling for the many fish species found in Salt Creek, such as channel catfish, largemouth bass, bream, crappie, and carp. The park, renamed after a longtime public servant, is also a popular picnicking destination. Visit three picnic areas on your hike and pass several others on the drive to the trailhead. The park also has a 0.75-mile jogging trail in addition to the Salt Creek Trail.

This particular hike explores the northern half of the Salt Creek trail system. The nearly level path leaves the canoe launch and works its way along the edge of Salt Creek, sometimes getting very close on sheer bluffs. At other times it's a little back from the waterway, but either way you will be getting good aquatic views of the stream with its gravel bars and shoals. Become well acquainted with the bottomland hardwood forest that accompanies the stream. Here ash, silver maple, cottonwood, hackberry, and other deciduous trees create a dense green canopy in summer. Some of these trees are huge. Stinging nettle and other brush occupy the forest floor. This light understory combined with the tall trees allows for extended views into the forest, which offers a kaleidoscope of color in fall.

Miles and Directions

0.0 Leave the Salt Creek Canoe Launch North, and pick up the Salt Creek Trail southbound. Salt Creek will be to your left. Walk along the stream just a short distance, and then turn away, circling around a tributary.

0.1 Emerge at a picnic area. Stay left, soon returning to Salt Creek. Resume cruising along the large stream.

0.2 Stay left again at an intersection. The mown path leading right makes a short loop.

0.4 Stay left as a trail leading right shortcuts the main loop.

0.5 Look on the left side of the trail for a huge sycamore. Watch for big cottonwoods, too.

0.6 Return to Salt Creek and follow it as the waterway curves back south.

0.8 Stay left at another trail junction, which shortcuts the loop.

0.9 Reach another trail junction. Keep forward and emerge at another auto-accessible picnic area. This is at the lowermost end of the north access road. The balance of the Salt Creek Trail continues south to the south park access. This is your decision point. You can either backtrack along Salt Creek, follow the access road back to the trailhead, or go back using the interior trails away from Salt Creek. The following

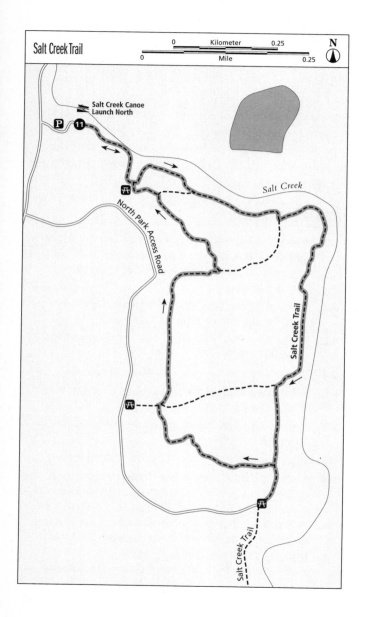

Salt Creek Trail

Salt Creek Canoe Launch North

P 11

Salt Creek

North Park Access Road

Salt Creek Trail

Salt Creek Trail

N

0   Kilometer   0.25
0   Mile   0.25

works through the interior trails back to the trailhead. Head north from the picnic area, and then turn left at the first intersection.

1.2 Reach a four-way intersection. A short spur leads left to a picnic area. A trail leaves right back to Salt Creek. Keep straight, heading northbound through bottomland hardwoods.

1.5 Curve sharply east. Stay left at the next intersection, now heading northwest.

1.7 Continue northwest as a trail leaves right.

1.8 Finish the loop portion of the hike after emerging at a picnic area near the trailhead. Backtrack.

1.9 Return to the trailhead and the Salt Creek Canoe Launch North, completing the hike.

12 Lakeside Nature Trail

This trail at Weldon Springs State Park circles a scenic spring-fed lake. Along the way you will enjoy good views of the 29-acre impoundment, as well as stopping by fishing platforms, crossing the lake dam, and visiting sobering Veterans Point. The trail visits the park marina and campground. Numerous ups and downs make for a fun hike and watery views are almost constant. While hiking the trail, note that this recreation area has been in operation for almost 150 years.

Distance: 2.0-mile loop
Approximate hiking time: 1.0 to 2.0 hours
Difficulty: Moderate
Trail surface: Natural surfaces, gravel, and concrete in places
Best season: Mar through Nov
Other trail users: None
Canine compatibility: Leashed dogs permitted

Fees and permits: No fees or permits required
Schedule: Sunrise to sunset
Maps: Weldon Springs State Park Trails; USGS Maroa
Trail contacts: Weldon Springs State Park, 4734 Weldon Springs Road, Clinton, IL 61727; (217) 935-2644; www.dnr.illinois.gov

Finding the trailhead: From exit 100 on I-55 northeast of downtown, take IL 54 east 40 miles to Clinton and a stoplight intersection with US 51. Turn right on US 51 south and follow it for 1.5 miles, and then turn left on US 51 Business north. Follow it 0.2 mile, then turn right on Revere Road. Follow Revere Road for 1.0 mile, then turn right on Spidle Road. Follow Spidle Road for 1.2 miles, and then turn left into the recreation area. Immediately turn right toward Veterans Point. Follow this park road for 0.4 mile, reaching the parking for the Schoolhouse Trail on the right side of the road. The parking for the

Lakeside Nature Trail is on the opposite side of the road from the Schoolhouse Trail and parking. GPS Trailhead Coordinates: N40° 7.090' / W88° 55.459'

The Hike

Weldon Springs State Park has been hosting families for hikes, campouts, fishing, and swimming since before the state of Illinois ever had a parks system. Back in the 1850s, a man named Lawrence Weldon purchased the land that is now the state park. People began coming to the springs as a recreation destination, but the area didn't take off until Weldon grouped with some other citizens to improve the site as a summer meeting ground. (A lake was developed but later expanded to the one you see today.) Here, citizens paid a fee to listen to public speakers waxing eloquent on a variety of educational, political, and historical topics. The gathering was known as the Chautauqua. For 20 years families and individuals camped out, engaging in physical and mental recreation. Later, the gatherings waned in popularity and the son of Lawrence Weldon sold the meeting grounds to the city of Clinton, which eventually deeded it to the state of Illinois. Weldon Springs is now a designated state recreation area and, given the 150-year history of Central Illinoisans coming here, recreation area is the proper term.

Not only are there hiking trails at Weldon Springs, but there are plenty of other activities to enjoy. You have the lake itself, popular for angling. The most popular catches are largemouth bass and catfish. Children will often be seen catching small sunfish from one of the many fishing platforms situated all along the lakeshore. You will see these platforms on your hike. Boaters can also fish and will be seen plying the 29-acre lake in rental boats and their own craft.

For the sake of peace and quiet, only electric motors are allowed. You might want to consider bringing a meal along with you, as the recreation area is dotted with picnic areas throughout the park.

This hike starts at a small picnic area. If you don't feel like cooking, you will actually walk by a full-service restaurant on the edge of the lake, which also serves as a marina to rent boats and sell bait. The camping here is pretty good, too. They have 75 sites that have electricity among other amenities. Showers are also available. After your hike, you will pass many of these park features and gain an improved understanding of just what is available here at Weldon Springs.

Along the lake spur trails stray from the main path. Most lead to either a fishing platform or the nearby park road. Lake views open time after time. You will shortly emerge at the lake dam. After crossing it, the next major highlight is Veterans Point. This is a memorial to soldiers who have defended our country's freedom. It is a moving sight. As you curve around the north side of the lake, pass an interesting wildlife carving. Here, a bald cypress tree that died served as the canvas for a chainsaw carving by one Paul Hoffman. Beyond here you will come to the concession area, where boats are for rent and you can grab a meal. The up-and-down trail then curves over to the west side of the lake. Skirt along the shore with the campground above the path. You may get a whiff of wood smoke and campfire cookery. The trail finally makes its way back around to the south side of the lake and the trailhead.

Miles and Directions

0.0 From the picnic area across from Union School, walk toward the lake on a concrete path, passing grills, picnic tables,

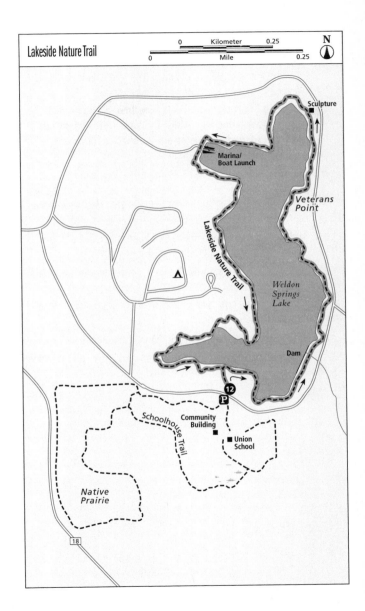

Lakeside Nature Trail

Kilometer
0   0.25

Mile
0   0.25

N

Sculpture

Marina/
Boat Launch

Veterans
Point

Lakeside Nature Trail

Weldon
Springs
Lake

Dam

12
P

Schoolhouse Trail

Community
Building

Union
School

Native
Prairie

18

and a restroom. Shortly, pick up the Lakeside Nature Trail and turn right, heading counterclockwise around the lake.

0.2 Emerge at the lake dam and spillway. Continue circling around the east side of the lake. Drift into woods, passing fishing platforms and small picnic areas.

0.6 Come to Veterans Point. Twenty-five tons of granite were used to create the memorials. The names of veterans are inscribed throughout the memorial, flags are flown. It is a serene spot.

0.8 Reach the wooden wildlife sculpture to your left. Ahead, bridge a stream, and then curve around an embayment and emerge on a point that offers perhaps your best view of the lake.

1.1 Pass the marina, restaurant, and boat ramp. Curve to the south on the west side of the lake.

1.4 Begin a long section with the park campground to your right through the trees.

1.6 Curve into the final lake embayment. Ahead, bridge a wet-weather stream.

2.0 Complete the loop. Backtrack through the picnic area where you started, finishing the hike.

13 Schoolhouse Trail

Explore a restored Central Illinois prairie as well as a wetland and a pair of historic buildings here at Weldon Springs State Park. The Schoolhouse Trail is a big birding destination, with several bluebird boxes scattered along its length. Much of the hike travels the nexus between prairie and woodland and thus you get to explore both environments. The wetland area offers another chance to enjoy bird life. Finally, explore a pair of historic buildings, including the Union School built in 1865 and the Texas Township Community Building, which was moved here two decades ago.

Distance: 1.5-mile loop
Approximate hiking time: 1.0 to 1.5 hours
Difficulty: Easy
Trail surface: Natural surfaces, mostly grass
Best season: Mar through Nov
Other trail users: None
Canine compatibility: Leashed dogs permitted

Fees and permits: No fees or permits required
Schedule: Sunrise to sunset
Maps: Weldon Springs State Park Trails; USGS Maroa
Trail contacts: Weldon Springs State Park, 4734 Weldon Springs Road, Clinton, IL 61727; (217) 935-2644; www.dnr.illinois.gov

Finding the trailhead: From exit 100 on I-55 northeast of downtown, take IL 54 east 40 miles to Clinton and a stoplight intersection with US 51. Turn right on US 51 south and follow it for 1.5 miles, and then turn left on US 51 Business north. Follow it 0.2 mile and turn right on Revere Road. Follow Revere Road for 1.0 mile and turn right on Spidle Road. Follow Spidle Road for 1.2 miles, and then turn left into the recreation area. Immediately turn right toward Veterans Point. Follow this park road for 0.4 mile, reaching the parking for the

Schoolhouse Trail on the right side of the road. GPS Trailhead Coordinates: N40° 7.085' / W88° 55.482'

The Hike

Central Illinois was once covered with forest and naturally occurring prairie lands. Since then, it has been mostly turned to agriculture, benefiting our country and the citizens of Illinois with food and a way to make a living. However, as time went on people began to realize that we should preserve a portion of the naturally occurring landscape as it was. Thus, you have places like the southwest side of Weldon Springs State Park where rolling terrain has been restored to native prairie, bringing along the flora and fauna that thrives within it. Native prairie land can be quite beautiful and not just a grassy field. Anybody who has seen the asters, bluestems, coneflowers, and other flowering plants will attest to that.

On this hike you will enjoy traveling through the prairie and also the wetland. This is not a naturally occurring wetland. A small dam was built, which slows the flow of an intermittent stream, creating a small pond surrounded by cattails. It attracts its own life from amphibians to birds. But the real eye catcher on this hike is probably Union School. The 150-year-old educational building was moved to Weldon Springs from Logan County, Illinois. It was in service for over eight decades. Today, the schoolhouse serves as a visitor center and classroom for children who come out on field trips. Within its confines you can learn all about the history of Weldon Springs, a gathering place for outdoor enthusiasts for as long as the Union School has been in existence.

Bring a hat and sunglasses as much of the trail is in the open. Your hike starts within sight of the historic buildings,

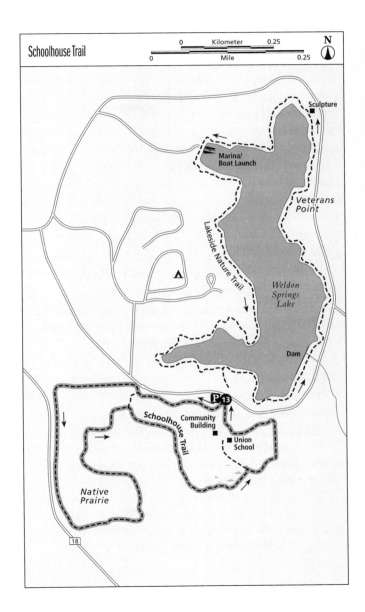

Schoolhouse Trail

Kilometer 0 0.25
Mile 0 0.25

N

Sculpture

Marina/
Boat Launch

Veterans
Point

Lakeside Nature Trail

Weldon
Springs
Lake

Dam

P 13

Schoolhouse Trail

Community
Building

Union
School

Native
Prairie

18

but I suggest saving them for last. Instead, pick up the School-house Trail traveling counterclockwise. In order to maximize the trail mileage, the path skirts the edge of the park property, rolling through restored prairie. Summer is a good time to come here as the flowers will be blooming. Either way, you will see much bird life. The area has also been enhanced for the avian set with bird boxes. The path also visits forests, presenting shady contrast to the prairie. After passing the wetland, you can then enjoy the buildings, though they may be closed during the week. Call ahead for hours in which the buildings are open to make sure you can enter. Otherwise, you may have to be satisfied with an external view only.

Miles and Directions

0.0 As you face the Union School, take the Schoolhouse Trail, leading right, or west, on a mown path through restored prairie.

0.1 The trail splits. A shortcut goes left, you stay right, coming shortly to another split. Here, a very short trail goes to the park road. Stay left, still hiking west.

0.3 The path turns south. You are now on the park boundary.

0.5 Turn back east. The forest closes in.

0.7 Turn north.

0.8 Emerge back into prairie.

1.0 Pass the other end of the shortcut trail. Continue on the margin between prairie and forest.

1.3 Reach the wetland and cattail pond. A trail goes left to the historic buildings. Stay right, continuing the circuit. Shortly, cross a closed park access road. The mown path curves left and heads toward the historic buildings.

1.5 Reach the historic buildings and complete the hike. Explore the buildings and grounds at your leisure.

14 Fairview Park Hike

This hike follows an asphalt greenway through one of Central Illinois' most historic parks—Fairview Park in the town of Decatur. You will start on its east end and work your way through the grounds, visiting sites and facilities both old and new. Large trees shade your walk through manicured grounds. The trail will leave the main part of the park, and then pass through a narrow tunnel of green to emerge near Stevens Creek. The trail then bridges Stevens Creek and comes to a picnic area and the end of Fairview Park. On your return trip you can explore such things as Dreamland Lake and the location where prospective Union soldiers mustered before the Civil War.

Distance: 3.0-mile out-and-back
Approximate hiking time: 1.5 to 2.0 hours
Difficulty: Moderate, due to distance only
Trail surface: Asphalt
Best season: Year-round
Other trail users: Joggers, bicyclists
Canine compatibility: Leashed dogs permitted

Fees and permits: No fees or permits required
Schedule: Sunrise to sunset
Maps: Decatur Bike/Walking Trails; USGS Decatur, Harristown
Trail contacts: Decatur Park District, 620 East Riverside Avenue, Decatur, IL 62521; (217) 422-5911; www.decatur-parks.org

Finding the trailhead: From exit 133A on I-72 east of downtown Springfield and on the west side of Decatur, take US 36 east for 3.2 miles, then turn right at the light at Eldorado Street. Follow Eldorado Street just a short distance to a second light. Now, turn left on Fairview Avenue and follow it a short distance, and then turn right on

Dreamland Lake Road. Follow Dreamland Lake Road for one block, and then turn right into Fairview Park. Cross the asphalt trail and reach a parking area on your right, just after crossing the asphalt trail. GPS Trailhead Coordinates: N39° 45.827' / W89° 40.499'

The Hike

Interestingly, the original site of Fairview Park was purchased by the city of Decatur to hold its annual Decatur/Macon County Fair. The gathering was held here for a number of years. Then it began being used full time as a park in the year 1890. Over the ensuing century plus the park has undergone many a transformation and its current use shows facilities both old and new. And some old facilities have become new again—Dreamland Lake, for example.

The hike is fairly easy with but a few hills. The asphalt trail is divided in the middle with a white line, ostensibly for bicyclers. However, most users seem to be ordinary hikers and joggers, as well as a few dogs walking their owners. And there's plenty to look at, especially if you've never been here before. First thing you'll notice are the huge trees. The park is dotted with massive hardwoods—cottonwood, maple, ash, oak, and more. Picnic tables are scattered under the trees and beckon you to stop.

You will come to a spur leading left to Rotary Pavilion and Dreamland Lake. This historic pond was revitalized. The lake had fallen into disrepair. In 2007 a woman's body was pulled out of the lake. She had been murdered. The ensuing publicity and uproar around the killing ultimately resulted in the refurbishment of Dreamland Lake and the grounds around it. The Rotary Club of Decatur donated substantial dollars to the pavilion. Today, you will often find people fishing in the small body of water bordered by attractive

Fairview Park Hike

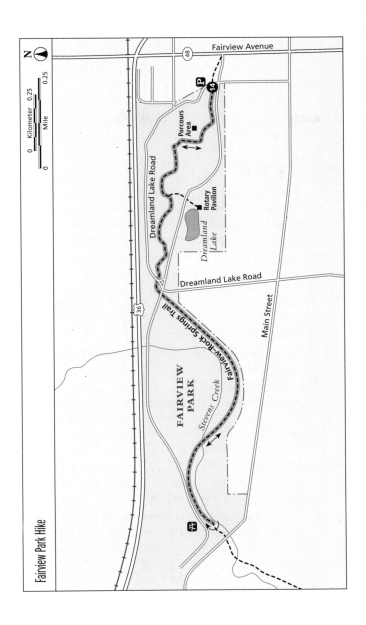

landscaping. The path leaves the main body of Fairview Park and crosses Stevens Creek. Here, it reaches the west end of the park, accessible from Main Street. At this point, you will find a picnic pavilion and benches. Stevens Creek flows on to meet the Sangamon River. This hike, however, turns around and heads back to the trailhead and the east side of Fairview Park.

Miles and Directions

0.0   Pick up the Fairview–Rock Springs Trail as it travels west into the heart of Fairview Park. A short segment of the trail goes the other way to Fairview Avenue. Immediately, you will see some massive old-growth trees rising above the mown lawn.

0.2   Pass a Parcours fitness center. Individual stations are set up with suggested exercises. Ahead, you will pass a band shell and play areas. Look for the monument where Union soldiers were mustered for the Civil War. In 1880, a Union soldier reunion was held here, and was attended by general and later president, Ulysses S. Grant.

0.4   The trail splits. The spur leads left to the Rotary Pavilion and Dreamland Lake.

0.7   Pass a small electrical station, and then bridge the continuation of Dreamland Lake Road. The trail next passes through a narrow, wooded corridor. The pathway backs up to yards on the left and the steep drop-off of the wooded valley of Stevens Creek on the right.

1.2   Cross Stevens Creek on a high pedestrian bridge. Descend to bottomland along the creek. In the future the 4-mile Stevens Creek Trail will head north up the Stevens Creek Valley.

1.5   Come to a picnic area with a pavilion and benches. The greenway continues straight and under Main Street to end at Rock Springs Conservation Area and Nature Center. Backtrack.

3.0   Reach the trailhead, completing the hike.

15 Fairview–Rock Springs Trail

This asphalt path travels by many highlights on its way from Rock Springs Conservation Area to Fairview Park. Leave the Rock Springs visitor center and travel through prairie, passing a pond. You undulate through rolling terrain, and then dip into lush bottomland forest dominated by silver maple. Enjoy the watery views from the bridge over the Sangamon River. You will then continue in extremely wooded lowlands cruising along Stevens Creek. The hike ends at a bridge over Stevens Creek. Your return trip will provide more potential fauna and flora sightings.

Distance: 3.4-mile out-and-back

Approximate hiking time: 2.0 to 2.5 hours

Difficulty: Moderate

Trail surface: Asphalt

Best season: Year-round

Other trail users: Joggers, bicyclists

Canine compatibility: Leashed dogs permitted

Fees and permits: No fees or permits required

Schedule: Sunrise to sunset

Maps: Rock Springs Conservation Area; USGS Harristown

Trail contacts: Macon County Conservation District, 3939 Nearing Lane, Decatur, IL 62521; (217) 423-7708; www.macon countyconservation.org

Finding the trailhead: From exit 133A on I-72 east of downtown Springfield and on the west side of Decatur, take US 36 east for 0.3 mile and turn right at the light at Wyckles Road. Follow Wyckles Road for 2 miles, and then turn left on Rock Springs Road. Follow it for 1 mile and turn left on Brozio Lane. Follow Brozio Lane for 0.1 mile and turn left onto Nearing Lane. It dead ends at the parking area near the visitor center. Pick up the Fairview–Rock Springs Trail on the far side

of the visitor center from the parking area. GPS Trailhead Coordinates:
N39° 49.449' / W89° 0.839'

The Hike

The Fairview–Rock Springs Trail connects two outdoor
icons in Decatur—Fairview Park and Rock Springs Conservation Area. Fairview Park is a century-plus-old outdoor
getaway that is part of the fabric of Decatur. Fairview Park
has a long history of recreational use. Rock Springs Conservation Area is a newer outdoor entity with different
characteristics. While Fairview Park has been solely based
on outdoor recreation, Rock Springs is more of a nature
preserve and an environmental education center with passive
outdoor recreation as part of its mission. It seems only fitting
that a pathway would connect these two parks.

The Fairview–Rock Springs Trail is part of a growing
network of interconnected paved paths running throughout
Decatur. This one is popular and deservedly so. It has easy
trail access on either end, and in between travels through
the valley of the Sangamon River in a wild setting. Walkers,
hikers, joggers, bicyclists, and even fishermen use the path.

There's no need to hurry onto the trail when starting at
Rock Springs. There is so much to see and do here, from
visiting the historic Homestead Prairie Farm to having a
picnic on the attractive grounds and checking out the visitor center. There is also an interconnected network of short
interpretive nature paths that will enhance your apprecia-
tion for Rock Springs Conservation Area. Try to build in a
little time either before or after your hike to soak in these
offerings.

Trail mileages are laid out in quarter-mile increments.
Resting benches are scattered along the way. Upon leaving

Rock Springs, you will pass through a prairie and a fishing pond. At this point the trail is mostly level with slight undulations. There are numerous trail intersections, but since this is the only paved path, it would be almost impossible to get turned around. You will dip into the bottomland of the Sangamon River. This is when the forest creeps up alongside and overhead of the trail. The long iron bridge over Sangamon River is a good place to stop. You will overlook deep bottomland that is often flooded in spring. When this occurs, the trail is closed, hence the gate you see before reaching the Sangamon River. Stevens Creek offers its own aquatic beauty. You will get a chance to enjoy a top down view of this waterway from its bridge. This is a good place to turn around, but if you wish to continue, there are two options as the trail splits beyond the Stevens Creek bridge. You can either keep straight to Fairview Park or turn right and head to Kiwanis Park.

Miles and Directions

0.0 Join the asphalt Fairview–Rock Springs Trail leaving west from the visitor center. Enter a stand of tall pines, remnants of a Christmas tree farm. Pass the Woodland Trail and the Discovery Trail. Your way opens onto restored prairie.

0.1 The Fairview–Rock Springs Trail curves right after passing more spur trails splitting away. Turn northeast.

0.3 Pass a pond on your right, separated from the trail by a fence.

0.4 Reach an access trail to the aforementioned pond. The short path leads to a wooden fishing platform on the north side of the impoundment.

0.7 Come to the first of two junctions with the River Trail.

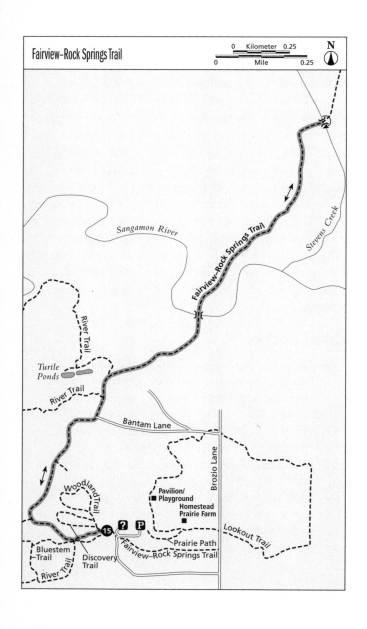

Fairview-Rock Springs Trail

0   Kilometer   0.25

0   Mile   0.25

N

Sangamon River

Stevens Creek

Fairview–Rock Springs Trail

River Trail

Turtle Ponds

River Trail

Bantam Lane

Woodland Trail

Brozio Lane

Pavilion/ Playground

Homestead Prairie Farm

15

?

P

Lookout Trail

Bluestem Trail

Discovery Trail

Fairview–Rock Springs Trail

Prairie Path

River Trail

0.8 Pass through a gate that is closed when the Sangamon River is flooded. Enter bottomland, rife with willows, silver maples, and other moisture-loving trees.

1.0 Bridge the Sangamon River. Ahead, come within sight of Stevens Creek. Watch for flood evidence—driftwood piled against trees, overflow channels, wet depressions, and mud astride the trail.

1.7 Come to a bridge over Stevens Creek just after passing a pond on your left. Enjoy looking at this stream before turning around and backtracking toward Rock Springs.

3.4 Complete the hike after returning to the visitor center.

16 Lookout Trail

This hike takes place at Rock Springs Conservation Area. You will enjoy Central Illinois human and natural history on this shorter trek. First visit the Trobaugh–Good House, a historic antebellum prairie homestead. Learn a little bit about life in pre–Civil War Illinois. The Lookout Trail next takes you through a prairie. Walk through native grasses on rolling hills before returning to full-blown woodland. The final part of the hike leads to a small stream in deep woods before returning to the trailhead. The conservation area has other trails and facilities that will enhance your visit.

Distance: 1.3-mile loop
Approximate hiking time: 1.0 hour
Difficulty: Easy
Trail surface: Natural surfaces, mostly grass
Best season: Year-round
Other trail users: None
Canine compatibility: Leashed dogs permitted

Fees and permits: No fees or permits required
Schedule: Sunrise to sunset
Maps: Rock Springs Conservation Area; USGS Harristown
Trail contacts: Macon County Conservation District, 3939 Nearing Lane, Decatur, IL 62521; (217) 423-7708; www.macon countyconservation.org

Finding the trailhead: From exit 133A on I-72 east of downtown Springfield and on the west side of Decatur, take US 36 east for 0.3 mile, and then turn right at the light at Wyckles Road. Follow Wyckles Road for 2 miles and turn left on Rock Springs Road. Follow it for 1 mile, and then turn left on Brozio Lane. Follow it for 0.1 mile and turn left onto Nearing Lane. It dead ends at the parking area near the visitor center. The Lookout Trail starts in the southeast corner of the parking area. GPS Trailhead Coordinates: N39° 49.449' / W89° 0.839'

The Hike

Rock Springs Conservation Area was initially acquired by Macon County in 1969. Since then it has become a place where human and natural history is preserved, where citizens of Central Illinois can learn about nature and explore a large tract of land on the Sangamon River, including uplands away from this flowing waterway. This particular hike first visits the Trobaugh-Good House, a restored homestead prairie farm listed on the National Register of Historic Places. The house and adjacent grounds replicate what life was like in this area prior to the Civil War. The house as you see it was first built as a one-room log cabin by Joseph Trobaugh, who hailed from Tennessee but came here to marry his Illinois wife. He and his family lived here for 13 years. He added on and altered the house, which was natural for a man who ran a sawmill in addition to being a farmer. Later it was lived in by others, namely a fellow named Good. It is not only the house you can visit but also outbuildings and a garden.

The hike then leaves the significant homestead and explores an Illinois prairie. The prairie you will visit was thick woods when Trobaugh arrived in the area. He cut the forest down and converted it to cropland, which was cultivated for a long time. Later, after the area was acquired by Macon County, prairie establishment took place. Creating prairie is not a one-time deal. Native grasses were planted in the prairie, but the ecosystem is also periodically improved through fire management. Walk through the rolling meadows with tall grasses and flowers galore in summer. At one time there was a lookout tower here, which is what lent its name to the trail. The lookout is no longer here, but there is plenty to pique your interest. Finally, the trail leaves the prairie and explores rolling hardwood hills before returning to the parking area, which also has cattail ponds, a picnic shelter and play area, as well as the visitor center.

Consider timing your visit with a living history demonstration at the Trobaugh-Good House. The park has special events centered on the homestead. Check the conservation area website calendar for upcoming events and times when the house is open for visitation.

Miles and Directions

0.0   Pick up the Lookout Trail on the opposite side of the parking lot from the trail to the visitor center. You'll see a sign for Homestead Prairie Farm/Lookout Trail. Follow an old lane into woods.

0.1   Come to the historic Trobaugh-Good House on your left. Take the time to explore the grounds. The house is open for visitation during certain periods. The Prairie Path comes in from the south.

0.2   Reach and cross Brozio Lane after leaving the historic house and continuing east. Enter prairie. Imagine Joseph Trobaugh working this land using farm implements of the mid-1800s. In summer, prairie grasses will rise high, bordering the mown path.

0.5   The trail continues east then reaches a patch of woods. Turn north, still in prairie bordered by forest to your right.

0.7   The Lookout Trail turns left, in a westerly direction, and then cuts through a wooded strip before opening to more meadow.

0.8   Pass a closed challenge course on your left.

0.9   Cross a closed service lane.

1.0   Cross back over to the west side of Brozio Lane, and then cut to the south side of Bantam Lane. The conservation area

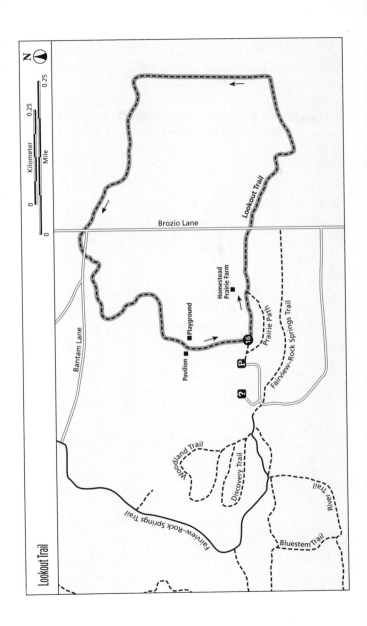

Lookout Trail

N

0   0.25   Kilometer
0   0.25   Mile

Bantam Lane

Brozio Lane

Lookout Trail

Pavilion

Playground

Homestead
Prairie Farm

P

16

2

Prairie Path

Fairview–Rock Springs Trail

Woodland Trail

Discovery Trail

Fairview–Rock Springs Trail

Bluestem Trail

River Trail

maintenance shop is within sight. Trace a grassy track into the woods, descending.

1.1 Bridge a streamlet at the bottom of the hill. Cruise dense hardwoods in a hollow.

1.3 Emerge onto the north side of the primary developed area. You are near a play area and pavilion. Walk south through the area to reach the trailhead shortly, ending the hike.

17 River Trail

This challenging yet rewarding hike travels the far reaches of Rock Springs Conservation Area. Leave the visitor center and hike over prairie and past a pond. Dip into thick riverside woods and come to the historic Rock Springs Bottling Plant. Next visit the site of a mill on the Sangamon River. Then the River Trail takes you to remote river bottom on the Sangamon, where silver maples grow by the thousands among wet-weather channels and seasonal overflow ponds. Enjoy multiple views of the river, finally turning away to visit the Turtle Ponds. The trail surmounts drier hardwood uplands rife with huge oak trees on its way back to the trailhead. Overall, the trail system at Rock Springs is well marked and maintained, allowing you to focus on the attractive scenery.

Distance: 3.6-mile loop
Approximate hiking time: 2.0 to 2.5 hours
Difficulty: More challenging due to elevation changes and changeable footing
Trail surface: Natural surfaces
Best season: Year-round
Other trail users: None
Canine compatibility: Leashed dogs permitted

Fees and permits: No fees or permits required
Schedule: Sunrise to sunset
Maps: Rock Springs Conservation Area; USGS Harristown
Trail contacts: Macon County Conservation District, 3939 Nearing Lane, Decatur, IL 62521; (217) 423-7708; www.macon countyconservation.org

Finding the trailhead: From exit 133A on I-72 east of downtown Springfield and on the west side of Decatur, take US 36 east for 0.3 mile, and then turn right at the light at Wyckles Road. Follow Wyckles

Road for 2 miles and turn left on Rock Springs Road. Follow it for
1 mile, and then turn left on Brozio Lane. Follow it for 0.1 mile and
turn left onto Nearing Lane. It dead ends at the parking area near the
visitor center. The River Trail starts on the far side of the visitor center
from the parking area. GPS Trailhead Coordinates: N39° 49.449' /
W89° 0.839'

The Hike

You have to pass the visitor center to begin the hike. Bud-
get in some time to see the displays and all the interpretive
information here. They also have programs going on year-
round, so it's worth checking into them as well. The hike
works through and past short nature trails clustered around
the visitor center. One you will be on is the Bluestem Trail.
It saunters through the restored prairie.

Reach Rock Springs, the Sangamon River, and the site
of the Rock Springs bottling plant. Visiting Rock Springs
has been a Macon County tradition since the 1800s, when
visitors would picnic in its vicinity. In 1907, a local educator
named Charles Parker bought a 40-acre farm that included
Rock Springs. Parker built the bottling plant visible today.
The springhouse is toward the river and behind the bottling
plant. Parker sold the water in 5-gallon crated bottles. He
stayed in the water business until his death in 1916. When
the Macon County Conservation District bought the land,
they closed and stabilized the bottling plant as it remains
today.

Your next venture into Macon County history is Millers
Mill site. Also built on the banks of the Sangamon, the mill
was established in the 1830s. The shallow Sangamon doesn't
naturally favor turning a mill wheel, so Miller built what is
known as a low head dam. This is simply a dam that rises but

a bit over the river at normal flows. The dam backs up the river to allow a constant minimum depth to turn the mill wheel and excess water simply flows over the dam. The dam was built by staking logs into the bottom of the river at low flows and building it up.

Watch for signs of flood while dipping into the bottom-land along the Sangamon River. This is a wild area of the park and subject to change from periodic high water. Absorb great views of the waterway before returning to the upland forest and the Turtle Ponds. The final part of the trail leads through forest and field back to the visitor center.

Miles and Directions

0.0 Start the River Trail by joining the asphalt Fairview–Rock Springs Trail leaving west from the visitor center. Enter a stand of pines, passing the Woodland Trail and the Discovery Trail.

0.1 Turn left on the River Trail, which at this point runs in conjunction with the Bluestem Trail. Roam south through grasses, and then turn west.

0.2 Pass a pond on your right, and then turn left at a junction, descending west, hiking along a line of trees.

0.4 Pass a corner post, and then dive into full-blown woods descending on a gravel track. Ahead, bridge a creek twice in succession. Massive white oaks rise in the forest.

0.6 Reach an intersection. Here, the Big Oak Trail keeps straight, while the River Trail leads left.

1.1 Reach the Rock Springs Bottling Plant and the Sangamon River. Now turn upstream along the Sangamon.

1.3 The spur trail to Millers Mill leaves left to a vista overlooking the Sangamon. The main trail climbs.

1.4 Meet the Big Oak Trail again. Stay left.

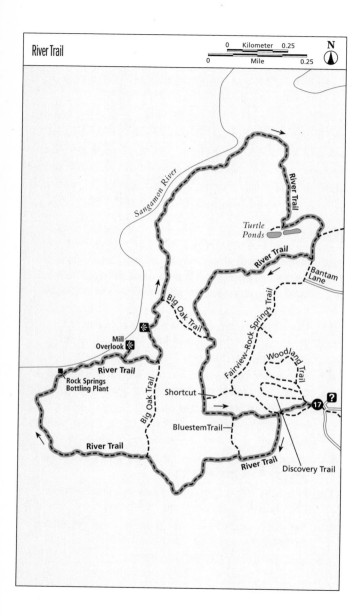

River Trail

0 Kilometer 0.25

0 Mile 0.25

N

Sangamon River

River Trail

Turtle Ponds

River Trail

Bantam Lane

Big Oak Trail

Mill Overlook

River Trail

Rock Springs Bottling Plant

Big Oak Trail

Fairview–Rock Springs Trail

Woodland Trail

Shortcut

17

Bluestem Trail

River Trail

River Trail

Discovery Trail

1.5 Reach a spur that leads left to a river overlook with a contemplation bench. Leave the upland woods for bottomland.

1.6 Keep straight on the River Trail as the Big Oak Trail leads right. The trail junctions end for a while as you take a single-track path through an impressive riverside forest.

2.5 Leave the bottomland and come to the Turtle Ponds.

2.6 Briefly join the Fairview–Rock Springs Trail, turning right, and then quickly leaving right from the asphalt path back onto natural surface trail, heading west.

3.1 Once again meet the Big Oak Trail. Keep south in forest.

3.3 Open onto prairie. A shortcut trail leaves left. Keep straight, and then curve left, going east.

3.4 Reach an intersection in the prairie. Keep straight, running in conjunction with the Bluestem Trail.

3.5 Complete the loop portion of the hike. Rejoin the Fairview–Rock Springs Trail heading toward the visitor center.

3.6 End the hike at the visitor center.

18 Griswold Conservation Area Vista

Enjoy a view of four counties from atop Blue Mound, located within the boundaries of the Griswold Conservation Area. This small preserve, encircled by farmland, presents a chance for nature to thrive and for you to walk through it. First, leave a picnic area then travel through woods and prairie to enter the north side of the conservation area, which is a wildlife sanctuary. You will then hike through a mix of prairie and forest before entering the dark woods of a demonstration windbreak. The trail then curves back toward the high point of Blue Mound, located atop a glacial kame. From here an observation deck allows views in almost all directions, stretching as far as the clarity of the sky allows.

Distance: 1.6-mile out-and-back
Approximate hiking time: 1.0 hour
Difficulty: Easy
Trail surface: Natural surfaces
Best season: Year-round
Other trail users: None
Canine compatibility: Leashed dogs permitted

Fees and permits: No fees or permits required
Schedule: Sunrise to sunset
Maps: Griswold Conservation Area; USGS Stonington
Trail contacts: Macon County Conservation District, 3939 Nearing Lane, Decatur, IL 62521; (217) 423-7708; www.macon countyconservation.org

Finding the trailhead: From exit 96 on 55/72 take IL 29 south to Taylorville and Main Cross Street at a traffic light. Turn left and follow Main Cross Street 0.1 mile to turn left onto IL 48 north. Follow IL 48 north 13 miles to Blue Mound. Turn left on Blue Mound Road, located just south of a granary. Cross the railroad tracks and stay straight, driving for 0.7 mile to Meridian Avenue. Turn right on

Meridian Avenue and follow it for 0.3 mile to the right turn into the Griswold Conservation Area. Follow the main road past the primary parking area on your left and then curve left past the maintenance shop to park in the Rotary Grove Picnic Area, which has a picnic shelter and restrooms. GPS Trailhead Coordinates: N39° 42.2498' / W89° 8.1561'

The Hike

The observation point you'll be hiking to atop the glacial kame is 706 feet in elevation—the second-highest point in Macon County. The hill rises 80 feet above the flat agricultural lands around it. Once atop the observation deck, you can look down and see not only the views from afar but how the gravel that comprises the glacial kame has been mined. Kames are formed by receding glaciers. Gravel in the meltwater gathers and leaves a mound. Much of the extrication of gravel was done during the Great Depression when the Civilian Conservation Corps came to this area and did local road improvement using the pebbly rock. Now, visitors are asked to stay off the remnants of the glacial kame, remaining on the trail and enjoying the feature leftover from the Wisconsin Ice Age from the overlook only. Of course, you can see this hill rising from all directions. And the hike here nearly encircles the rise.

The hike starts at the Rotary Grove Picnic Area. Take note of the large stone monument commemorating the picnic area's establishment. Begin your circumnavigation of the glacial kame above. The slight elevation of the trail allows for far views beyond the conservation area, into agricultural lands stretching to the horizon. The wildlife sanctuary portion of the conservation area is more wooded. All too soon you are turning up the grassy hill to make the overlook.

The views atop the mound are stunning. The naturally occurring woodlands immediately below contrast vividly with the row-cropped agricultural lands beyond. Adjacent villages can be seen as well. To the south of the observation deck you will note a long, grassy, mown hillside. This part of the hill is kept mown for good sledding in winter. It is a short and simple walk back to the Rotary Grove Picnic Area, but it will cut your mileage in half. Go ahead and backtrack, making the full mileage and enjoying the conservation area further. Also, a half-mile tree-lined grassy trail leads east from the conservation area to the village of Blue Mound, should you want to stretch your legs a little more.

Miles and Directions

0.0 From the Rotary Grove Picnic Area parking, walk north past the picnic shelter and restrooms, to a grassy trail entering woods. Walk amid pines and hardwoods, emerging shortly into mixed meadow and trees. The slope rises to your left. As you walk along, the elevation is high enough to gain a far-reaching perspective of agricultural fields to the east. You can also look back at the village of Blue Mound.

0.2 The path turns west, passing through a hardwood pine grove that is a demonstration windbreak. These windbreaks slow the blowing of the wind, cutting down on windborne erosion.

0.4 The trail turns south.

0.6 Come to a willow- and cypress-bordered pond. Curve east.

0.7 Pass the main developed facilities of the conservation area. A short spur trail leads right and connects to the trail you are on. This is the way most people climb to the observation area. Begin the uphill tick to the overlook.

0.8 Reach the observation deck perched on the edge of the glacial kame. Just below you is the dug-out gravel pit. Views stretch to your north, west, and south. The easterly view is

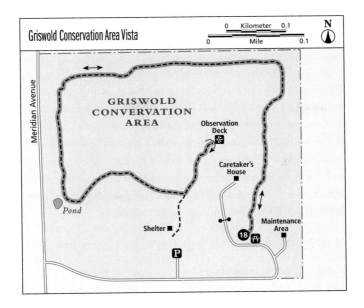

partially blocked by trees, but they may be cleared in the future.

1.6 Complete the hike after returning to the Rotary Grove Picnic Area.

19 Lincoln Prairie Trail

This rail trail runs between Taylorville and Pana. This section starts at Lake Taylorville and travels north. You will follow a level asphalt track up a wooded corridor, spanning a creek on a trestle. The hike continues to the larger bridge over Flat Branch, a tributary of South Fork Sangamon River. Soak in stream views before turning back.

Distance: 3.2-mile out-and-back
Approximate hiking time: 1.5 to 2.0 hours
Difficulty: Moderate
Trail surface: Asphalt
Best season: Year-round
Other trail users: Joggers, bicyclists
Canine compatibility: Leashed dogs permitted

Fees and permits: No fees or permits required
Schedule: Sunrise to sunset
Maps: Lincoln Prairie Trail; USGS Taylorville
Trail contacts: Taylorville Tourism Council, PO Box 13, Taylorville, IL 62568; (217) 824-9447; www .visittaylorville.com

Finding the trailhead: From exit 96 in Springfield on I-55/72 east of downtown, take IL 29 to Taylorville. Stay with IL 29 through Taylorville to reach Main Cross Street and a traffic light. (There will be a sign here indicating a left turn to IL 48.) Set your odometer here and continue straight on IL 29 toward Pana. Drive for 1.8 miles to Lake Road and the entrance to Lake Taylorville and Kiwanis Park. Turn right here and stay right on West Lakeshore Drive to park immediately at Kiwanis Park. GPS Trailhead Coordinates: N39° 31.846' / W89° 15.032'

The Hike

Central Illinois is all things Lincoln. So it is no surprise a rail trail is named after the area's most prominent historical figure. True, Abe was a circuit-riding lawyer who passed regularly through Taylorsville, so it isn't really a stretch to name this rail trail for him. This path was completed in a cooperative effort between the cities of Taylorville and Pana, as well as the Illinois Department of Transportation. It follows an abandoned rail line. Ultimately, plans call for the trail to extend 45 miles from Pana to Springfield. The trail segment between Pana and Taylorville was opened in 2001. This hike travels two of the four bridges along the route. The Lincoln Prairie Trail extends for 12-plus miles south from this trailhead to Pana, and 2-plus miles north to Taylorville. Consider hiking part of the trail and bringing your bicycle for a longer exploration of the Lincoln Prairie Trail.

Leave the Lake Taylorville area, heading north on the railroad grade. A tunnel of green soon envelopes the pathway, blunting the auto noise from IL 29, which runs parallel to the Lincoln Prairie Trail. The hiking is easy as there is virtually no elevation change. You are roughly following the South Fork Sangamon River before it makes a big curve to sweep around the west side of Taylorville, then flowing to meet the main stem of the Sangamon on the southeast side of Springfield.

Beyond the first trestle, woods thicken to your left. Ample hardwoods grow branch to branch. The old railroad grade cuts into a hill, creating an intimate environment. Notice sassafras growing tall along this path. Sassafras trees are easy to identify. Their leaves have three basic shapes: oval, three-lobed, and mitten-shaped. Mature sassafras trees have a reddish-brown, deeply furrowed bark. The trailside trees here are big enough to have the furrowed bark. Sassafras trees are known for their aromatic scent. Scratch the bark away from a twig and the sweet smell is unmistakable. American natives

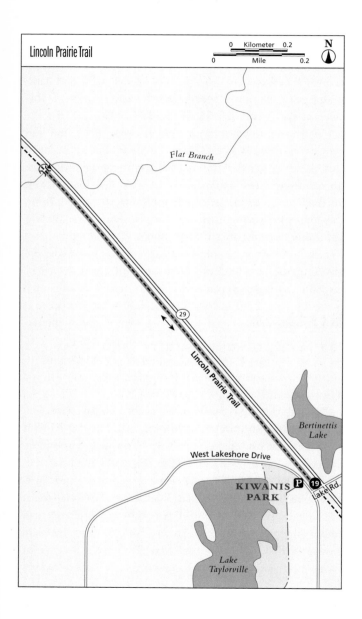

Lincoln Prairie Trail

used sassafras for medicinal purposes. Pioneers, and even people today, make tea from boiling sassafras roots. Birds eat the berries. The wood of sassafras shrinks when dried and is used for fence posts and hand tools. Oak, maple, sycamore, sassafras, and walnut add to the species list. This deciduous variety makes a colorful autumn walk.

Continue through the long, green tunnel. The land falls away upon nearing Flat Branch. You will see light ahead upon approaching the Flat Branch trestle. From the trestle you can look down on the flowing waters of Flat Branch shortly before they merge into South Fork Sangamon River. This is a good turnaround point. It is one mile farther to Taylorville from the Flat Branch trestle. After getting a taste of the Lincoln Prairie Trail, you may want to contact the Illinois Department of Transportation and urge them to expand this path all the way to Springfield.

Miles and Directions

0.0 To get the full mileage, walk from the Kiwanis Park parking area back where the Lincoln Prairie Trail crosses the entrance road adjacent to IL 29. Begin heading northwest up the old railroad grade toward Taylorville.

0.2 Cross the first trestle. The outflow of Bertinettis Lake flows below, to meet Lake Taylorville. Lake Taylorville is created by the damming of the South Fork Sangamon River.

1.0 A residential road crosses the rail trail. Keep straight.

1.1 The trail passes under a power line.

1.6 Reach the Flat Branch trestle. This tributary of the South Fork Sangamon River flows east to west under the bridge. This is a good place to turn around.

3.2 Complete the hike after returning to Kiwanis Park.

20 Hickory Lane Trail

Situated at water-oriented Sangchris Lake State Park, this forgotten path leaves the state park campground, exploring uplands rising from the South Fork Sangamon River. The jungle-like trail delves deep in the forest, sometimes on the slope above the South Fork. Finally, the trail emerges back in another part of the campground. At this point you can walk the campground roads back to the trailhead, or backtrack on the footpath.

Distance: 2.4-mile out-and-back
Approximate hiking time: 1.5 to 2.0 hours
Difficulty: Moderate
Trail surface: Natural surfaces
Best season: Year-round
Other trail users: None
Canine compatibility: Leashed dogs permitted

Fees and permits: No fees or permits required
Schedule: Sunrise to sunset
Maps: Sangchris State Park; USGS Edinburg
Trail contacts: Sangchris Lake State Park, 9898 Cascade Road, Rochester, IL 62563; (217) 498-9208; www.dnr.illinois.gov

Finding the trailhead: From exit 96 on I-72/55 southeast of downtown, take IL 29 south for 4.7 miles to Cardinal Hill Road. Turn right on Cardinal Hill Road and follow it for 5.3 miles to a stop sign and New City Road. Turn left on New City Road and follow it 4.3 miles to enter the state park. Set your odometer at the state park entrance sign and continue driving 1.1 miles to the left turn into Deer Run Campground. Trace the main campground road for 0.4 mile to the Hickory Lane Trail and parking area on your right. GPS Trailhead Coordinates: N39° 39.270' / W89° 28.103'

The Hike

It is completely understandable that Sangchris State Park would emphasize water recreation above all. After all, if it weren't for the creation of Sangchris Lake in 1964, the park wouldn't be here. Commonwealth Edison dammed Clear Creek to make a 3,000-plus acre lake, providing water for cooling at its nearby power plant. The state began using 1,400 acres of shoreline for recreation and it later bought a portion of the lakeshore in 1997. The park service developed the facilities in a big way with boat ramps, fishing platforms, picnic areas, cabins, two campgrounds, and also a few trails. Frankly, the hiking trails seem to have been put on the back burner. However, there is still a path called the Hickory Lane Trail that emanates from the Deer Run Campground. It provides a deep woods hiking experience. It once was also an interpretive trail, but that seems to have fallen by the wayside. The trail in its current state is still followable, and presents an opportunity to hike here at Sangchris Lake State Park. Perhaps you could combine your hike with some fishing, or especially camping, since the trail begins and ends at the Deer Run Campground. In fact, campers stumbling onto the trail hike it more than people coming here to deliberately give it a whirl.

The hike begins as a singletrack footpath entering a dense canopied forest. Locust, oak, walnut, dogwood, sassafras, and of course, hickory are just a partial list of trees you'll find here. Among trees, this trail offers significant vegetational variety. After passing a trail intersection, the main loop descends a little bit to bridge a streamlet. This is the first of numerous small bridges that span intermittent drainages leading down to South Fork Sangamon River. In summer the woods are so lush it seems a world away from the vast farmlands of Central Illinois. The South Fork Sangamon is near but visible only in winter.

Pawpaw trees grow in groves in the bottomlands of the South Fork Sangamon River. You will see them at low, moist points, forming an understory below the taller hardwoods. They are often found together in groups, since they reproduce by root sprouts. Pawpaws have large leaves, 6 to 12 inches in length, which droop like their tropical cousins farther south. Their yellow, banana-like fruit is favored by wildlife, especially raccoons and possums. Settlers made bread and puddings from pawpaw fruits. Attempts have been made to cultivate pawpaw as a fruit tree. Pawpaws grow throughout the Land of Lincoln where low, moist woods are found.

The trail continues along the point where the bottomland meets the upland hills. That combined with numerous bisecting wet-weather streamlets draining into the Sangamon results in plenty of ups and downs. When driving through the main part of the state park, you'd never know an ecosystem like this existed here! The path emerges at the primitive camping area At this point you can backtrack on the trail or follow the roads to the trailhead. If you follow the roads, just walk to the next road intersection and stay left. The road going right leads to the equestrian camp. The road going left pops out shortly onto the main campground road. Stay left here and you will reach the parking area in 0.3 mile. All the same, I would backtrack to get more exercise and take a double dip into nature.

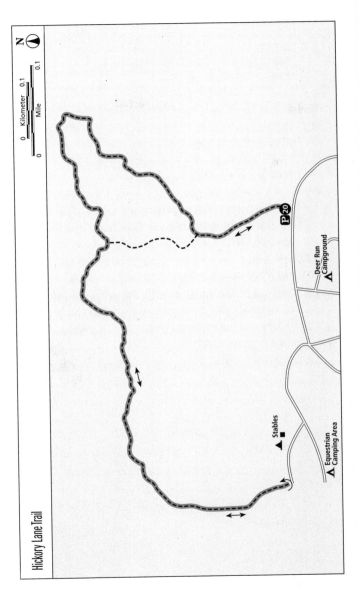

Hickory Lane Trail

Miles and Directions

0.0 Join the Hickory Lane Trail as it heads north away from the Deer Run Campground. Another spur trail comes in from the trailhead parking area.

0.1 Come to a trail intersection. The path leading straight makes a short loop. Stay right with the main outer circuit.

0.2 Cross an intermittent streambed on a wooden bridge. Another wooden bridge lies just ahead.

0.4 Pass a duck moss–filled pond to the right of the trail. Beyond here the trail turns sharply west.

0.6 Reach a trail intersection after climbing a steep hill. The other end of the short loop leaves left. Stay straight, continuing west, and descending toward bottomland where paw-paws grow thick.

0.7 Pass a huge oak just after crossing a boardwalk bridge. The trail continues undulating and crossing streamlets.

1.0 Pass another big oak on your left. The trail curves away from the South Fork Sangamon and closer to Clear Creek.

1.2 Emerge near the Primitive Camping Area. It offers restrooms and campsites. Backtrack.

2.4 Complete the hike, arriving at the trailhead.

About the Author

Johnny Molloy is a writer and adventurer with an economics degree from the University of Tennessee. He has become skilled in a variety of outdoor environments and written over forty books, including hiking, camping, paddling, and comprehensive regional guidebooks as well as true outdoor adventure books. Molloy has also written numerous articles for magazines, websites, and blogs. He resides in Johnson City, Tennessee, but spends his winters in Florida. For the latest on Molloy's pursuits and work, please visit www.johnny molloy.com.

AMERICAN HIKING SOCIETY

Because you
hike.
We're with you
every step of the way

American Hiking Society gives voice to the more than 75 million Americans who hike and is the only national organization that promotes and protects foot trails, the natural areas that surround them, and the hiking experience. Our work is inspiring and challenging, and is built on three pillars:

Volunteerism and Stewardship

We organize and coordinate nationally recognized programs—including Volunteer Vacations, National Trails Day ®, and the National Trails Fund—that help keep our trails open, safe, and enjoyable.

Policy and Advocacy

We work with Congress and federal agencies to ensure funding for trails, the preservation of natural areas, and the protection of the hiking experience.

Outreach and Education

We expand and support the national constituency of hikers through outreach and education as well as partnerships with other recreation and conservation organizations.

Join us in our efforts. Become an American Hiking Society member today!

American
Hiking
Society

1422 Fenwick Lane · Silver Spring, MD 20910 · (800) 972-8608
www.AmericanHiking.org · info@AmericanHiking.org